A guide to

BANKING IN BRITAIN

A guide to

Banking in Britain

ROBIN PRINGLE
Editor of *The Banker*

with a Foreword by Lord Cromer
former Governor of the Bank of England

CHARLES KNIGHT & CO. LTD.
LONDON
1973

Charles Knight & Co. Ltd.
11/12 Bury Street, London EC3A 5AP
Dowgate Works, Douglas Road, Tonbridge

This work first appeared in *Systèmes Bancaires d'Europe Occidentale (hors C.E.E.)*, published for the Institut d'Etudes Bancaires et Financières by Dunod, Paris, in 1970

ISBN 0 85314 192 4
Printed in Great Britain by
Brown Knight & Truscott, London and Tonbridge

Contents

List of Tables

Foreword

by

Lord Cromer,

Former Governor of the Bank of England

In the following pages appears a most lucid and succinct account of the British Banking system. There are few experts on banking who will not find some morsel of information that is new to them. Within its compass, this account is probably the most complete and most factually informative work on the British banking scene to have been published.

The author begins his study by a brief appraisal of the development of banking within the British legal system, in so far as it is concerned in this field, and then seeks to describe the growth of banking in Britain within the perspective of the country's commercial and financial history. He discerns, correctly in my opinion, that the establishment of London as an international financial centre, wherein half of the deposits in the banking sector are for account of non-residents of the UK, has been largely due to freedom from detailed banking legislation.

From this Mr. Pringle proceeds to an account of the workings of the "clearing banks", the emergence of the big units of today, with their various ancillary activities followed by some intriguing vignettes of the individual banks, which through mergers have led to the pattern that exists today of the "Big Four".

Similar treatment is afforded the "merchant banks" who have continued to thrive throughout the centuries largely due to their adaptability and their flair to meet the changing needs of changing times, again unhampered by restrictive banking legislation.

Then Mr. Pringle turns to the British overseas banks with their network of some 3,500 overseas branches scattered around the world. Although the bulk of this development coincided with the growth of the British Empire, there was considerable activity outside the Empire, particularly in Latin America. The growth of nationalism has in many parts impaired the contributions that could be made under the old system, as compared with the banking system still operated in many French overseas territories; but there are other areas with interesting future potential.

The foreign banks in London—there are over 200 of them—next receive attention as being essential elements in the City of London's claim to offer the most complete international financial centre. Then Mr. Pringle touches briefly on some of the ancillary financial institutions peripheral to the banking core.

The section which follows on the money markets, both those of traditional origin and the "new" markets such as the interbank market, and the ubiquitous "euro-currency" markets, and the manner in which these fit into the London financial scene is of particular interest.

Mr. Pringle concludes with an objective survey of monetary policy and the Bank of England, including a brief description of the organization of the Bank of England. Whilst, as an ex-Governor of the Bank, I would not be expected to endorse every word, this survey nonetheless strikes me as worthy of the high standard of this study taken as a whole.

Introduction

BANKING is one thing the British are rather good at, like politics. It may not seem so to the customer waiting in the queue to cash a cheque, just as the British talent for political compromise was scarcely evident in, say, Northern Ireland in 1972. Yet as Britain stood on the eve of entry to the Common Market, in January 1973, there were sadly few things that its future partners unreservedly admired in Britain, and its banking and political traditions were two of them. Its bankers, from chief executives down to junior bank clerks, were not only honest, relatively efficient and polite, in a society where these qualities were no longer so common as to pass unnoticed, but London's bankers were also seen to command formidable financial resources, world-wide connections and a large repertoire of skills and services. London was, and was expected to remain, the main banking centre of Europe and with New York one of the two biggest banking centres in the world.

That eminence, and the respect accorded it, were the results of a continuous development over three centuries. There may have been more bankers of individual flair and great fortune abroad, in Italy, Germany, Switzerland and the United States. It is true, too, that British banks no longer loomed so large on the world scene as they did when England was the world's dominant power. The banks themselves also today have many critics at home, who have been saying that the banks are not energetic and fast-moving enough. Yet banking has always flourished here, with its crises and its critics. There is something about the atmosphere of England, with its unusual mixture of conventional and informal behaviour, relative political stability, overseas adventurousness and financial honesty that made people here ready to lend or deposit money, between bankers and their customers, on a previously unimagined scale, both at home and overseas. For that is the real genius and the real contribution of the British to finance, readiness to lend, though many a customer in recent years, faced with a tight-fisted bank manager, can hardly be expected to have thought so. It was this readiness to lend that financed the industrial expansion of the later nineteenth century at home, and also helped to push the rest of the world on to that helter-skelter of economic growth from which it has yet to step off (though the British had second thoughts about the growth game long ago).

This book tries to give an account of that development, and the present banking system of Britain—domestic and international. But it is neither a celebration nor a critique of it. It does not convey, at least not intentionally, any ideas I have for the reform or improvement of British banking. It was originally written to describe banking to readers across the Channel, and I would be happy if it did anything to help increase our understanding, in this uniting (yet still so diverse) Europe of ours, of one aspect of each other's traditions.

A CATALOGUE OF COMPLAINTS

That having been said, it might perhaps be of interest to some readers if before the main text I list some of the criticisms that have been made recently, or not so recently, of British banking, without pretending in such a short compass to do any of them full justice.

1. First must come that class of criticism that derives essentially from the application of the *economic principles* of competition and free enterprise to the practice of banking (and monetary policy). Many of these are touched on in the body of the book, since they have had a direct impact on banking and the reforms that the monetary authorities and bankers have recently accepted. These criticisms attack all constraints, formal or informal, legal or merely conventional, that inhibit free competition between banks, and between banks and other financial institutions. Under this class of criticism would fall the various "gentlemen's agreements" on interest rates that banks should charge on loans and allow on deposits, (most of which were abandoned in September, 1971) and any practice that inhibits freedom of entry into banking. Critics alleged, with justice, that if only the banks competed fully with each other, many of the other features of banking that were coming under fire would disappear: the excessive number

of bank branches per head of population, *overstaffing* in some areas whilst the general level of staff salaries was too low, the sluggishness of the big banks to enter new fields of activity, their excessive (in some years) profits, their distorted interest rates (which long had the effect of subsidising the borrower at the expense of the depositor, who received a comparatively poor rate for his money), and their declining place in the financial structure of the country in the first 25 years after the last war. These arguments, which grew in force and intensity through the 1960s, were finally accepted and acted on in 1971, as described in the text. They have already (August, 1972) begun to have a great effect in galvanising the big clearing banks to greater activity (though the contrast with their previous mood should not be pushed too far), and in changing the structure of their interest rates to give greater fairness to depositors.

2. Secondly, there are those criticisms which derive basically from observation of *foreign banking techniques* and organisational know-how. American banks, in particular, are studied. Certainly the average level of disciplined knowledge about financial analysis and credit techniques, industrial practices and technology, is, in my view, superior in the great American banks to that in the British clearing banks and overseas banks—and even the merchant banks fall down sometimes, though their personnel are far better paid and generally more expert, in their specialities, than the staff in other British banks. It is true that the US tradition, and especially the European tradition, are different from that in Britain. European banks have always been close to industry, and even own large chunks of it, because in the absence of a market where industrial enterprises could raise funds directly from the public, the banks were the only source of finance both long term and short term (i.e. for capital investment as well as working capital, stock holdings, etc.). Thus they got to know about industry. Yet in my view critics are right in thinking that British banks may have to move in this respect slightly nearer their continental counterparts—not necessarily to put up much more money themselves for long-term investment, but to become intimately acquainted with industry and technology. This is mainly because the sheer size of the projects to be financed, the steadily growing scale of activity, and the complexity of huge industrial companies demands that even on pure banking grounds—so that they can assess lending risks—banks must develop greater technological capability. Even more important,

they must employ more academically trained people both as experts and as senior managers. At the time of writing, only one of the chief executives of any of the "Big Four" banks has a university degree (though the situation is different in other banks). Of course, the very genius of British banking has historically lain in quite non-academic qualities, qualities for which an academic background has been thought in England to be even detrimental: character and all that. It was, indeed, probably only amongst people who spent more time getting to know each other than thinking and reading that the sudden flowering of the readiness to lend—on a massive scale—would have occurred. And it was only when certain conventions were observed that such personal knowledge, and the trust that is built up with it, can yield firm and reliable patterns of behaviour. This is the reason and justification for the part played by conventions in British banking, and by quite "untrained" people. But the world of banking has yielded to rationalization like most others, and has been brought within the ambit of the "expert" with his typically disciplined—and even to him exciting—approach to affairs. These criticisms of British banking do the past less than justice, but are probably mostly right for today. So more experts, more industrial know-how, more management skills—and better pay.

3. Related often to this is the notion that the British banks should finance long-term *industrial investment* and take shares in companies on a large scale. But that is what the public does through the capital market, and does fairly efficiently. Bankers will doubtless do more to bring along smaller and medium-sized companies (especially as they get to know more about industry, see above) and if inflation carries on so crazily as in 1971-72, they will doubtless wish increasingly to acquire ownership of real assets—i.e. a share in company ownership. The large volume of long-term loans with which they are already in practice providing finance for fixed investment could be converted to equity stakes: if banks in effect take the risk, they should have some reward too. Most of the big banks have said they are prepared to do this. But as a long-term deliberate reform policy, it would carry few advantages and some risks; public confidence in banks could be put in jeopardy because an industrial company was in difficulties.

4. A quite different kind of criticism is that which alleges that Britain's participation in international banking has on balance harmed rather than benefited the country *economically*. There are two main varieties of this criticism, which is the first we have

encountered on this list so far that regards the system from outside as a whole, from a different set of assumptions than those held by bankers themselves:

4 (i). It is sometimes argued that the existence of such a finely developed international banking mechanism has encouraged people to invest too much overseas, both in the late nineteenth century and early twentieth century and again in the 1950s and 1960s. This meant that British industry was starved of investment capital, and started even as early as 1870 to fall behind in terms of modernisation of plant and equipment, and that overseas investment went to swell the dividends and interest income of rich widows in Eastbourne rather than men's employment income in Huddersfield. There has been much academic discussion about this, and in my view, the critics have come out slightly on top, though defenders of overseas investment remain quite convinced that the visible and invisible exports to which it gives rise, the technological feedback, the enlargement or protection of foreign markets, and the possible cheapening of imports make it economically as productive as comparable investment at home. What does seem to me to be unproven, is to assume (a) that savings prevented from being invested overseas would have been invested at home, and (b) that human welfare would have been increased if it had. After all, it is becoming surely out of date to take a purely insular view (though this came back to popularity between 1914 and about 1960), and on a global view, who can doubt that Britain's valiant outpouring of its savings has done more for world economic development and standards of living than if it had, indeed, all gone to Huddersfield? And where would the world be if every nation kept its savings all at home? If Britain is merely complaining that it did not receive enough gratitude from others for its self-interested but productive investment—and just got accused of being a colonialist exploiter—that is another story and another argument. That's something to leave to history. On this point, then, Britain's overseas investment, reflecting the same outward-looking mentality as its international banking ventures, was in my view, inevitable and right.

4 (ii). The second variety of this more fundamental criticism of banking is that it has made Britain chronically prone to currency crises, because the volume of our foreign currency reserves has always been so small in relation to our liabilities that any knock to confidence in the value of sterling gives foreign holders a

fright. Such is the dangerous life of an international banking country, a country that lends what it earns, and more—the reserve function of sterling (how it came to be held by other countries as part of their national reserves) is merely a sideline, a by-product of this banking role. In other words, we were borrowing short—foreign deposits being attracted to London by those wonderful money markets and the great convenience of sterling in world trade—to lend long. That was the old version. The modern version of this argument blames specifically our participation in Euro-dollar business: sometimes dollar deposits in London may be converted into and out of sterling, depending on relative interest rates and confidence in the two currencies, thus jolting our reserves. This goes together with the complaint that Britain's relationship with the sterling area and its whole "banking" mentality has made it too reluctant to devalue its currency when that was necessary. Actually, sterling was devalued in 1949, of course, and, though very persuasive, in my view a little more than is really justified has been made of this argument. Many other countries who have never played much part in the international banking game have been reluctant to change exchange rates—Germany and Japan for instance. And I personally wonder how many economic historians in a few years' time will attribute Britain's slow growth rate in the past generation (relative to other countries) in any large degree to its exchange rate policy. Finally, I do not think that it was the sterling area or banking function that was specifically responsible for the reluctance to change the exchange rate, even if that was important, but rather Britain's whole traditional stance in international affairs, its odd remaining feeling of responsibility for the world—which had once been its world. And again, to end with, some countries like France have always liked to hoard their earnings in gold, the opposite of the banking instinct, but there was never any suggestion until the 1960s that this ever did any good to France's growth rate.

5. A really serious attack, again quite different, comes from those who blame the City of London and its banks for attracting too many of the nation's *bright boys.* (Girls are a recent intrusion into the City and have been kept away from, and below, the men's jobs: the prejudice is generally unconscious which makes it even more appalling. Socially some, only some, folk in the City still live in the 1920s.) For all that has been said above about "untrained" gentlemen in the banks, it is, I hope, not too para-

doxical if I say that there is probably a greater concentration of sheer ability, intelligence and knowledge about world affairs in the City of London than anywhere else in Britain, or even perhaps in Europe.

The charge is that the rich rewards, good life and frankly the snob appeal of the City has, down the years, attracted young people with ambitions (social or financial), like moths to a solitary flame. Starving Huddersfield again, this time of talent. The attack can be developed into a thoughtful critique of the role of services generally in the British economy—(a sector which started to grow fast and attract talent even 90 years ago)—bringing in the pernicious effect of the public schools in prejudicing "young gentlemen" against a life in trade or industry and the North of England generally, the traditions of the landed gentry, the temptations of running the British Empire at the expense of starving industry of managers, and so on. Personally, I have always thought these comments mainly justified. The City *has* a quite unfair proportion of intelligent recruits. But, looking back, wasn't it only for a very short time, in the early 19th century and the railway boom, that industry really caught the imagination of the English? And it is hardly realistic or constructive, however true it may be, to blame the English for not being keener on industry when in fact they prefer practising services such as finance, and adventuring overseas.

6. Another onslaught comes periodically from the *political* front. A mild form of this broke out at times when the last Labour government kept suffering from the delusion—for delusion it was—that international speculators in the City and abroad were gunning for it, aided and abetted by Tory bankers, a Tory press and various other villains in Labour's own cute chamber of horrors. It should not now be necessary for any fair-minded observer to repeat that banks and treasurers of internationally-mobile funds only react to situations and the expectations they give rise to. If it is a fact that Labour parties are expected to give higher priority to growth and social spending than Tories, and perhaps less to the exchange rate for sterling (before the Tories started floating the currency and all that), then the markets will quite impersonally register such an expectation. Politicians are supposed to know about facts and deal with them, not bleat about non-existent conspiracies. It was the Labour government which held then "old-fashioned" ideas about the sanctity of sterling, even if the Bank of England also naturally

regarded the exchange rate as a matter of great national importance. But the City of London generally was quite prepared, in 1964, when Labour came to power, to watch how the new ideas worked out, however much they disliked some of them and used legitimate influence to combat them.

This merges with the more obscure and important question of the influence generally of the City's views in political affairs and decisions—particularly when the Conservatives are in power. Against a determined Labour government there is really little the City can do—the trouble with the last one was that, like Labour governments before it, it was too deferential to what it thought were the City's views, and insufficiently determined to plug on with its own ideas. But a Conservative government is naturally friends with the City. Many leading bankers, as well, of course, as the Governor of the Bank of England in his official capacity, will know leading members of the Tory Government, including the Prime Minister, quite well. They meet in the evenings. They met and talked before he was elected. It is not necessary to go back to the Bank rate tribunal report in 1958 to realise the close links—family, school, and business experience—that have in the past connected the Tories and the City. Yet the mood at most such meetings is usually one of questioning. The City above all wants to be well-informed. It wants to know what politicians are doing, or are likely to do. That is the first step. Then on particular issues it will campaign, through Government departments like other lobbies, or by sending letters, which will be politely answered, or by making speeches, and it will then win or lose—on a new taxation detail, perhaps, or some new review committee. There will be hardly any matter on which it has any specially greater influence than any other lobby, the only difference being that City bankers, as is their custom and aptitude, work through personal talk rather than by submitting detailed reports to civil service departments like formal "lobbies" do (the BMA, NFU, etc.). Any idea that the City is ever given special information out of which it can make money directly, or that bankers in turn ever try to bribe ministers or officials, is quite childish. And the political influence of even the greatest merchant banker is, I would judge, nowadays less than that of, say, a regular television interviewer or a low-ranking trades union leader. The City is a background presence, that is all. So much for the conspiracy theory.

7. This political point should be sharply distinguished from

those criticisms that focus on *abuses* in the City itself—such as the use of "inside" knowledge to make profits on the stock exchange, which has happened on occasion and which should be made a criminal offence—or on laxness in governmental requirements concerning financial institutions, or laxness in the administration of those requirements. On such points, there is much to be said for more detailed legislation and this is indeed inevitable. Yet it is probably a necessary cost of a free society that there will always be a few who are able to ride on the fringes of lawful activity, and who cannot be gunned down without ending the freedom of all others. The City's legitimate interest is to minimize the openings for the few "spivs", whilst maximizing the freedom for its great banks and other institutions. And that is the country's interest too. For the City, after all, is its major single export industry (a statement that could be disputed by those who would take another definition of the word "industry", but which I regard as accurate); and the standard of living of all the inhabitants of Britain depends on such exports, whatever political and economic system is in force.

Without going to the far extreme of revolutionary Marxism, or moral outrage at anything to do with money, this list perhaps has shown some of the more common complaints made about bankers and the City. My own view is that, without widening the criticism to include English society and government at large, bankers fill their place in it on their own assumptions pretty efficiently. And every society needs some judgments system—it can never be purely automatic—for channelling savings into productive investment and credit for trade.

Part I
Character and Historical Development

It is usual these days to stress the rapid and accelerating pace of change in financial matters, just as in economic or political affairs. Keeping up with the latest financial techniques is thought to be what matters. The future is at a premium, the past at a discount. That is why this book starts by looking resolutely backwards, about 300 years back, with the following purposes in mind:

1. To help us distinguish those elements in the all-consuming present that may endure because they have roots, from those that may be merely transitory;
2. To reveal some of the character of British banking, as made up of the habits and experience of its bankers:
3. To find some interest in the story.

But before then, I shall jump to some conclusions and present baldly some of the features of the banking landscape that seem to me fairly permanent, unless the whole political and social situation takes a radically new turn.

WHAT REMAINS CONSTANT

Different authors would naturally stress different aspects of British banking. Most bankers would, however, agree that it has several distinguishing features: first, it is an *open system;* second, British banking as a system has never been *ordered or codified by statute;* third, it is domestically a *concentrated industry;* fourth, banking is almost entirely in the hands of institutions in the *private sector* of the economy; fifth, the credit techniques are still generally *simple and flexible;* sixth, banking activities have often been subject to certain *conventions,* either between the banks themselves or between the banks and the monetary authorities. The strength and restrictiveness of these conventions varies according to the circumstances and prevailing ideas of the time.

We shall look at each of these features in turn.

By an *open system* I mean that English bankers have always looked outwards, to the world beyond Britain's shores. This attitude predated Britain's short-lived experiment with Empire-building and has survived its demise. It also preceded the age of sterling's dominance as an international currency, and has survived sterling's inevitable decline. It is an attitude dictated by the facts of geography and population: English bankers have to be involved in international trade because England depends on such trade. But this open approach is also shown by the readiness to welcome foreign merchants and bankers to London. They have come, down the years, for many reasons; some have fled from religious or political intolerance, or war (such as the Huguenots in the seventeenth century or Jews in our own time); others have come just for business reasons. The forms of business they have established here have been equally varied; the early entrants, such as those that came during or after the Napoleonic Wars, often settled in England permanently; in this century, the tendency has been to set up branches or subsidiaries in London. Whatever the reasons and forms of business, they have found in England a relatively stable political structure and a relatively attractive business environment. To-day, there are more foreign or foreign-owned banks in London than English banks; deposits by non-residents represent more than half of all deposits with banks in England; finally, British banks still have the world's largest network of overseas branches. These three statistics are perhaps rather surprising; they illustrate better than anything else the international character of banking in England.

Another distinguishing feature of English banking is the *absence* of a formal statutory *banking law*. Description of banking in many other countries naturally starts from certain laws: as, for example, the laws of June 13, 1941, and December 2, 1945, in France; the law of July 10, 1961, and others, in Germany; the law of 1936 in Italy; the various decrees and laws in Belgium; and so on. Then one can describe how the system has evolved within the framework of these laws, and how these laws themselves come to be modified perhaps in the light of experience and changing circumstances. In England there are no such laws. Naturally bankers are affected by a number of general laws relating to the conduct of business (such as the Bills of Exchange Act, 1882, and the Cheques Act, 1957). But at least since the middle of the nineteenth century, there has never been a law laying down legal requirements on the kind of business that banks may or may not transact; or fixing prescribed cash or liquidity ratios; or restricting their ability to open branches; or making a separation between "deposit" and "investment" banking. There is not even any statute that defines what a bank is, or is not; even more oddly, there is no official complete list published of banks in England. There are only various lists published by the Department of Trade and Industry giving exemption from various requirements, and statistical classifications by the Bank. Generally speaking, however, a bank is a bank in the eyes of the law if it is accepted as a bank by the general public (and particularly by the City of London): that is, if it takes money on current account, pays cheques drawn by customers, collects cheques for customers and is generally accepted by "ordinary intelligent commercial men" as carrying on the business of banking. Banks certainly have several privileges. In particular, they are free of the restrictions of the Protection of Depositors Act on the use of the words "bank", "bankers", or "banking" in advertising, except for institutions recognised as "banks". They are also exempted from certain important provisions of the Companies Act, 1948; in effect, they need not publish their true profits, though the biggest banks have ceased to take advantage of this, and do publish true profits. If a company seeks these privileges, it must persuade the Department of Trade and Industry (DTI) that it ought to be treated as a bank. If any enterprise wants to advertise for deposits and call itself a "bank" or "banker", then again it must gain permission from the DTI. For foreign exchange business, Bank of England permission is required. The main point is, however, that there is no Act of Parliament defining banking, or regulating it, as there is in most other countries. There are no special legal restrictions on their activities.

Domestic banking in Britain is also highly *concentrated.* There are only four banking groups in England (and two in Scotland) which maintain large branch networks within the country: namely, Barclays Bank, National Westminster Bank, Midland Bank and Lloyds Bank; and, in Scotland, the National and Commercial Banking Group (which also owns an English bank, Williams and Glyn's), and the Bank of Scotland. Taken together, these banks dominate the field of "retail" banking. They account for about three-quarters of all bank deposits by British residents. They have altogether about 13,500 branches, employing approximately 200,000 people. They also have important interests in some British overseas banks, and, through subsidiaries, in hire purchase finance and many other activities. They are the giants of British banking. True they suffered from competition from other banks (and from institutions outside the banking sector) during the 20 years after the Second World War. But if this concentration has lent a certain rigidity to British banking, it has also given it stability: in England there has not been a major bank failure since 1920. The structure and work of the deposit banks is described in Part IIA.

It is also important to stress that virtually all commercial banking in Britain is conducted by profit-making companies in the *private sector* of the economy. The only bank in England ever to be taken over by the State is the Bank of England, in 1946. The only large group of financial institutions which could be described as part of the public sector are the savings banks, namely the National Savings Bank and the Trustee Savings Banks: both are parts of the National Savings movement and the funds they receive are invested in securities issued by the Government or UK local authorities. But they are not full "banks" because, at the time of writing, they are still not allowed to lend, their statistics are not included by the Bank of England as part of "the banking sector"; and although they have many thousands of branches and millions of accounts, they do not play a role in British banking comparable to the role of the savings banks in Germany, for instance. Their services are described briefly in Part IIE. The only other "bank" in the public sector is the Post Office Giro, but this is still small and, again, cannot lend money.

Turning to the techniques of credit in Britain, these are still, despite increasing sophistication of financial affairs, *simple* to understand and flexible in operation. The most common and popular method of short-term finance remains the overdraft, where the customer borrows by simply drawing on his normal current account up to a certain credit limit agreed between him and his banker. The customer pays interest only on the net daily overdrawn balance standing in his current account. The interest rate for most industrial and commercial borrowers is $1\frac{1}{2}$ per cent or 2 per cent over the bank's "base rate". (Before September, 1971, when the new competitive regime of credit control was introduced, bank lending and deposit rates were linked to Bank Rate.) Personal and other borrowers might pay 2-4 per cent over.

Finally, it is necessary to note the role historically played by *conventions* in English banking. These have been of two kinds: conventions agreed and upheld between the banks themselves (mainly the deposit banks), and those which may come to have the force of official requirements.

The most important *inter-bank* agreements have been formed amongst the deposit banks. In the past, they have agreed amongst themselves on the basic interest rates to be charged to customers on advances (which comprise about half their balance sheet total). By another convention, the clearing banks for many years agreed to offer customers only one rate of interest on "deposit" accounts, (called time deposits in other countries) which was ordinarily fixed at 2 per cent below the current level of Bank Rate, and there was only one type of "deposit" account—that for money requiring seven days' notice (in theory) of withdrawal. The merchant banks, overseas banks and foreign banks in London, as well as finance houses and others outside the banking sector, did not adhere to these agreements.

The most important conventions upheld by the monetary authorities relate to requirements that banks should hold certain types of asset (in proportion to their deposit liabilities). These had their origins in bankers' bitter experience, during the nineteenth century and previously, which taught them to keep a proportion of their assets in a form that could be easily mobilised in case of need. But for many decades, these conventions have served, primarily, to help the authorities to control the volume of bank deposits and advances, in the interests of overall economic policy. Until September, 1971, there were two main requirements on the clearing banks: first, that cash (that is to say, notes and coin *plus* balances with the Bank of England) should be kept to a fixed ratio to total deposits of 8 per cent; second, and in practice more important, that liquid assets (cash, money with the discount market, Treasury bills and commercial bills discounted) should be at least 28 per cent of total deposits; this latter was a *minimum* requirement, and in practice the banks' liquidity ratio was usually somewhat above this figure. Apart from these requirements, monetary policy relied heavily during the 25 years after the Second World War on "requests" and "moral suasion", i.e. demands by the authorities that the banks should limit their advances, or give priority to certain borrowers and so forth.

After September, 1971, the official requirements were changed as part of a radical switch in the method of credit control (see page 122); therefore all banks had to maintain a "reserve assets ratio of $12\frac{1}{2}$ per cent. Reserve assets were defined as including Treasury bills, commercial bills, Government securities with less than a year to run balances with the Bank and call money with the London money market. Cash holdings were excluded. The aim was to evolve a uniform set of requirements that would treat all banks equally and allow them to compete freely with each other—and yet enable the authorities to influence the volume of bank deposits held by the public, and so the money supply.

HOW THE SYSTEM EVOLVED

All these features are products of the past; of the political, economic, social and financial history of the UK. So any history of British banking needs to be informed by an intimate knowledge and analysis of Britain's general history. No such history can be attempted here. Nevertheless, even a brief outline may suggest which of the features of banking as it exists today are deep-rooted in the past, and which are of recent growth. This outline will therefore touch only on the main turning-points in the development of banking, in chronological order. Brief histories of particular institutions, notably the great clearing banks, are given in Part IIA, and of the foreign banks in Part IID. For the sake of simplicity, the outline is ordered by centuries.

THE SEVENTEENTH CENTURY

Although some rudimentary forms of banking had been practised in England since the fifteenth century (and indeed before), mainly by outposts of Italian houses, the roots of modern banking are usually traced back to the latter part of the seventeenth century.

A rapid development took place in the half-century after the Restoration of the monarchy in 1660—a period which, in so many ways, established the foundations of modern English history. It was the age of Isaac Newton, of scientific experiment, of the secularization of music, the development of the modern stage, of modern English prose with Swift, and of the first newspapers, and, in political thinking, the foundations of the liberal mode of thought. In the sphere of economic institutions, Britain's trade with all parts of the world was developing rapidly: with Turkey and Russia; Portugal and Greece; the Baltic and Africa; and particularly with the colonies such as those established in the West Indies (sugar), Newfoundland (fish), Virginia (tobacco) and 11 other American colonies, and the trading posts in India. A huge re-export trade developed, with goods bought from all over the world and re-sold to overseas markets mainly in Europe. The coal, iron, glass and silk industries, as well as the traditional clothing industry made progress. All these enterprises, at home and overseas, required large-scale organization and finance. So it is not surprising that this age also saw the development of joint-stock companies, and of the insurance, banking and shipping facilities that still today dominate the work of the City of London. Their evolution since that time has been continuous: that is to say, uninterrupted by any absolute break such as other European countries suffered, by invasion or revolution.

In banking itself, this period (1650—1700) saw two main developments: first, the transformation of some goldsmiths into bankers; second, the foundation of the Bank of England.

In the bustling commercial life of London there was naturally a growing need for safe places where merchants could keep surplus cash safely, and a growing demand for credit (loans). The goldsmiths came to provide both. They had for some time dealt in foreign currencies, keeping some in hand to supply people travelling abroad and melting down the rest as part of their goldsmith's trade. The goldsmiths' facilities for the safe-keeping of cash and valuable articles had also long been sought after, especially after Charles I had destroyed the reputation of the Royal Mint for this purpose by seizing £200,000 of safe-custody deposits in 1640. When Charles II came to the throne in 1660, it was therefore to the goldsmiths that he turned to borrow money to support his court and tortuous foreign policy. But the goldsmiths also lent money to their private customers. By the end of Charles's reign, in 1685, many of the techniques of modern banking were in common use; the goldsmith-bankers received money for safe-keeping, lending a proportion of these deposits to people needing finance: issued receipts for money deposited (which developed into bank notes): and accepted the written instructions of depositors (which developed into cheques). During this period, the immigration of some Protestants from France, after the revocation of the Edict of Nantes, and of some Jews from Spain, also probably helped financial development.

The Bank of England was established with a Royal Charter in 1694 and its immediate purpose was, yet again, to raise money for the Government from the rich merchants of London. But now William and Mary were on the throne of England, and the money was needed for a war against France and, in effect, for securing the Protestant succession to the throne: i.e. for causes that the merchants supported. Its capital of £1,200,000 was subscribed in six days, and the proceeds lent to the Government. The notes that the Bank was allowed to issue against receipts of the subscriptions are historically interesting, since they formed the beginnings of the "fiduciary issue", i.e. notes backed by Government securities. In other respects the Bank of England operated just like the goldsmith-bankers: it accepted deposits (and even paid interest on them), issued notes, and discounted bills of exchange with the aim of making profits. But the Bank was established by Act of Parliament; its credit was from the start bound up with that of the Government; and so it was a powerful competitor to the private banks (many of which opposed its establishment).

Of course the Bank had no thoughts then of becoming a central bank on the modern pattern. Yet some of its chief characteristics date from its foundation; in particular, it has always sought to maintain the confidence of the City, on the one hand, and yet also that of the Government, and, eventually, of the country at large. This has often been a difficult task, but seldom so difficult as in its first infant years. Some sections of the City itself feared that the Bank would grow too powerful, monopolize credit business, and show favouritism to certain merchants at the expense of others. It would become, they said, merely an instrument of State finance, allowing the King's Government to escape the control of Parliament (so a clause was inserted into the bill forbidding the Bank from lending money to the Government without the consent of Parliament). It was opposed by many landowners and other folk in the country as a mere instrument of high finance (which it was); by extreme Tories and Jacobites who thought it would help to consolidate the Protestant monarchy (which it did); and by those opposed to the very idea of a perpetual national debt (which it fostered).

In terms of the practical politics of the time, the main need was to satisfy the City and the Government. City "bankers" and merchants accepted it, on balance, because they thought it would be good for business and provide more secure banking facilities than were being offered by many goldsmiths; the Government needed the money. Personalities counted for much, then as now. The plan for the Bank was formulated by a clever, adventurous Scotsman, William Paterson; yet without the support of Michael

Godfrey, a rich merchant who gathered together many leading personalities in the City, and Charles Montagu, Chancellor of the Exchequer, on the side of the Government, the Bank might never have got off the ground. Once established, both sides came to realize that their larger interests were involved. Only this co-operation enabled it to survive the many crises of subsequent years. As the Chancellor of the Exchequer said in 1696, at a time of great financial difficulty for the Government:

> "The Bank, not withstanding all the hardships and discountenance they have met, are yet resolved to venture all for the Government and I hope what they do in our distress will not be forgotten in theirs if ever they are in a greater."

THE EIGHTEENTH CENTURY

English people often look back on the eighteenth century as a time of peace and quiet prosperity despite the wars abroad; as a time of pleasant country towns and fine family houses, when professional families, farmers, smaller landowners and some shopkeepers enjoyed increasing leisure, education and prosperity; when the power of the House of Commons gradually increased whilst that of the monarchy as gently declined, though both state and church were still utterly dominated by the aristocracy; a time, in short, of gentleness and enjoyment before the strains of mass industry and democracy.

Historians have frequently pointed to the omissions in this idealized picture; the wretched position of the agricultural labourer, the scale of corruption throughout the state, the frequency of riots. Certainly the first two decades or so of the eighteenth century were years of political and financial uncertainty: until the Peace of Utrecht in 1713, England was involved in a world-wide war against France and Spain. Yet it is clear that, in general, conditions nevertheless favoured the spread of financial and banking services, where the main developments were the further evolution of the Bank of England and the beginnings of "country banking".

The Bank of England was deeply affected by the war. It had to withstand several financial panics. Of more lasting importance, in 1708 the Government again turned to it for further finance to support the war. In return, the Bank's Charter was renewed, and it was granted a further extension of its monopoly.

An Act passed in 1697 had laid down that no other joint-stock bank should be allowed by Act of Parliament; but it had not forbidden the formation of other joint-stock companies. The new Act of 1709, however, *prohibited any company or partnership or any body of people exceeding six in number from issuing notes.* This clause had far-reaching effects on British banking: it was interpreted for more than 100 years as barring the formation of joint-stock banks in England and Wales (though they were allowed in Scotland, where banking therefore from the eighteenth century was in the hands of large joint-stock companies: the Bank of Scotland had been formed in 1695 and the Royal Bank of Scotland was founded in 1727). It was not realized until much later that deposit banking could be profitable and did not infringe the Bank of England's Charter.

The next danger for the Bank—apart from various Jacobite manoeuvres and plots—was the crash of the South Sea Company in 1720. This might easily have brought down the Bank, just as the fall of the India Company ruined the Banque d'Escompte in France. The South Sea Company had been formed in 1711 to fund a part of the State's large floating debt in return for a theoretical monopoly of trade in the Spanish dominions of Central and South America (though Spain in fact only granted a concession to trade there in 1713, and even then only one ship a year was allowed). By 1720 the Company's ambitions were such that it proposed taking over the entire National Debt (of some £31 millions); rashly, the Bank of England offered to take over the debt itself on absurd terms. But these proposals, fortunately for the Bank, were rejected. The South Sea Company's plans were given Parliamentary approval, and its stock began its historic leap, from £126 to £2,000. A crazy speculative fever gripped the community; dozens of fraudulent schemes were promoted; corruption and bribery on the normal vast eighteenth century scale ensued. When, in the end, the doubts took root, the Bank promised, again rashly, to help the Company. But the public panic had started; the Bank repudiated its agreements, and survived.

During the remainder of the century, the Bank gradually consolidated its position, not only as the Government's bank, but also increasingly as the bankers' bank. The private bankers of London naturally disliked the competition, especially from the Bank's notes which were slowly coming into widespread use (in 1725 the Bank made the first general issue of bank notes bearing printed amounts—for £20, £30, £40, £50 and £100). But they increasingly found it convenient to bank their own surplus balances with the Bank.

The other development at this time was in "country banking". In keeping with the growing prosperity of towns outside London, some merchants and shopkeepers in the country were beginning to offer banking services as a subsidiary business (they set up another "department", so to speak), on the pattern of the London goldsmith in the previous century. They took safe-custody of cash and valuables, issued notes and made loans; the best of them were men who were not only trusted in the community where they worked, but who had also a keen judgment of the amount they needed to keep in cash and "liquid" assets and the purposes for which they should lend. This was, of course, as in America to-day, a "unit banking" system; branch banking was virtually unknown (in England and Wales). The Bank of England's monopoly prevented the formation of larger units. As the industrial revolution began to press on the supply of credit, and there was increasing demand for acceptable paper currency, the weaknesses of many of these "country" banks were revealed—especially as a great number came to be founded. In 1750 one contemporary source said there were not more than 12 "bankers' shops" outside London; by the 1790s the number had probably grown to between 300 and 400; and in 1810 to over 700. There were several waves of bank failures, especially after the beginning of the war with France after the Revolution; not only did many country banks fail, partly due to their own faults, but in 1797 the Bank of England itself was forced to suspend convertibility for several years.

The beginnings of London's discount market can also be traced back to the "bill brokers" of the eighteenth century. The country banking system we have outlined was *localized* banking and localized banking in districts that, from the nature of their economic life, provided the banker either with an excess of deposits for which no local use could be found, or with an excess potential demand for borrowing. In the early stages, country bankers more commonly experienced an excess of deposits, and often found employment for these funds simply with their banking agents in London. But they soon came to employ the services of "bill brokers" instead.

THE NINETEENTH CENTURY

The century opened with a succession of financial crises; these were caused partly by the lack of large banks brought about by the Bank of England's monopoly, partly by defective organization of the banks, partly by the strains of the Napoleonic wars and of the industrial revolution which was transforming the country's economy. Despite this, the financial system was able to tap the rapid increase in real wealth and enabled the Government to finance vast expenditure on the war with relative ease.

The most severe crisis came in 1825, when about 70 fair-sized banks were forced to stop payment. The clamour for ending the Bank's "monopoly" grew.

In 1826, Parliament passed an Act which allowed joint stock banks to be formed outside a radius of 65 miles from London; that is to say, outside the area dominated by the Bank of England note. The Bank of England was jealously fighting for its privileges as a commercial bank; and in this matter it was supported by the London private banks, which feared that joint-stock banks would become strong competitors for them (and they were right). In 1833, however, another Act of Parliament was passed which permitted joint-stock banking throughout the United Kingdom. These two Acts were promptly followed by the foundation of several bigger banks. As the short sketches of bank histories in Part IIA show, the large banks of to-day often date from this period.

The private bankers fought hard against the "new" banking of the joint-stock banks. It was only in 1854, for example, that joint-stock banks were admitted to the Clearing House. But gradually joint-stock banks increased their strength and began to absorb the private banks. They also started to provide some ancillary services beyond the scope of the private banks. The extension of the principle of limited liability to banking gave them a further stimulus. The joint-stock banks themselves began to amalgamate. In 1866 there were 246 private banks and 154 joint-stock banks (with 850 branches). In 1900 there were only 19 private banks left, compared with 77 joint-stock banks (with 3,757 branches). This process was carried a decisive stage further in 1918-20, when the "Big Five" banks emerged (all joint-stock); after that, there was no further change amongst the big banks (with the exception of National Provincial's take-over of the District Bank and a few other affiliations) until the major mergers of 1967-69. These latest mergers have left only four big banks to provide the bulk of England's "retail" banking services (see below).

The growth of the big deposit banks in the nineteenth century was associated with several changes in financial habits. First, the chief method of transferring money within Britain came to consist in the *transfer of bank deposits* effected by the written instructions of the debtor to his bank, i.e. the use of cheques came to predominate over the use of coin and of bank notes and of bills of exchange. Second the *bank overdraft* gradually replaced the discounting of bills of exchange as the predominant source of short-term credit. Associated with this, thirdly, the channelling of funds within the country from the "agricultural" areas (with a surplus to lend) to the "industrial" areas (net borrowers) came to take place largely *within the branch banking* system rather than through the intermediary of bill brokers in London. From 1854 the "clearing" of cheques between banks took place at the Clearing House, and any net indebtedness of one bank to another was settled through drawing a cheque on its account at the Bank of England in favour of the other bank (as still happens) rather than by the transfer of bank notes, and this greatly reduced the demand for bank notes.

All these changes were connected together. At the same time, there was an increase in the number of people opening bank accounts. Until the middle of the nineteenth century, banking was still confined to the wealthy classes; even bank notes were generally issued in too large denominations to be of much use in day-to-day transactions.

The nineteenth century also saw the development of *other kinds of banks* besides the clearing banks; these were notably the merchant banks, British overseas banks and the savings banks.

The *merchant banks* often started, as did the "country banks", from merchants who developed a "banking" side to their activities; only in this case, the merchants specialized in the finance of international trade. Gradually, the range of their business widened to include bill acceptance, share issues and other activities. Traditionally many of the directors of the Bank of England have come from merchant banking. A fuller account of the development of merchant banks is given in Part IIB. British *overseas banks* were founded from the 1830s onwards, to develop banking business in Australia, India, Africa and South America: these banks began to reproduce in countries of the Empire a branch banking system such as existed in England (see Part IIC).

The *savings banks* were originally philanthropic institutions, designed to provide savings facilities and encourage savings (in true Victorian fashion) among poor people. But many of them were badly managed; and as the movement grew, there was increasing concern as to its control, and there were successive Acts of Parliament to regulate the operations of the banks. In 1861, the Post Office Savings Bank was set up, but the other savings banks continued to be popular and still provide competition for the clearing banks (although it was only in 1965 that they won the right to issue cheques, and their deposits are not counted as part of the money supply).

The *discount market* reached the apex of its power and importance in the latter part of the nineteenth century. Its earlier role, as a channel of funds from agricultural "surplus" areas to industrial "borrowing" areas of the country, had been made redundant by the development of branch banking. The bill of exchange as an instrument of domestic finance declined. Instead, the discount market came to occupy other key functions in the banking system. First, commercial banks developed the habit of keeping call loans with the discount market as their first line of reserves. Second, it came to be accepted that it was only to the discount houses that the Bank of England would lend "at last resort", but that it would lend to them without fail in times of crisis. Third, the discount houses came to provide the market where the massive volume of sterling bills of exchange, drawn by traders all over the world, could be discounted; they financed this operation often with funds placed on deposit with them from overseas. This is one way in which the level of interest rates in the London money market came to have such an important influence on international banking in the nineteenth century and on the flow of funds to and from London. By raising Bank Rate, the Bank of England could make London a less attractive place to borrow and a more attractive place to invest; the pull was such that, as they said, 7 per cent would draw money from the North Pole and 10 per cent would draw it from the moon.

Meanwhile, the *Bank of England* gradually developed most of the attributes of a modern central bank and also became the pivot of the international financial system based on the gold standard. We have seen that the Bank had a special position in the country's banking system from the date of its foundation. Right from the beginning, the Government had accepted that it should stand by the Bank in times of strain : it was the only bank in England established by Act of Parliament and the main instrument for raising funds for the State; it also undertook for the Government the circulation of Exchequer Bills, the management of the issue of Government securities and, from 1751, the administration of the National Debt. But in most other respects it had acted just like another commercial profit-making bank.

During the nineteenth century, the Bank's activities as a central bank gradually came to predominate over its direct banking services to non-bank customers. An important stage was reached with the Bank Charter Act of 1844. This laid down that no new bank in the United Kingdom could issue notes and placed restrictions on existing note-issuing banks (it said that any bank that amalgamated should lose its rights to issue notes) with the clear intention that the Bank of England should eventually have a monopoly. This had far-reaching effects: it further stimulated the development of deposit banking; it caused the commercial banks (private and joint-stock) gradually to keep their central reserves at the Bank of England; by the same token, it in effect gave the Bank responsibility for managing the currency. But the implications of this for monetary policy were not fully understood for a long time.

How was the Bank to manage the currency? Victorian ethic dictated that it should be by rigid principles, though there were many people, even then, who argued that the Bank should have discretion to vary the note issue according to the needs of industry. The Act of 1844 laid down that the "fiduciary issue" (the issue of notes backed by securities and not by gold) should be limited to a fixed amount, and that all notes issued in excess of that sum should be fully backed by gold. Bank notes were therefore virtually gold certificates. And it went without saying that the over-riding aim of policy was the maintenance of the fixed gold value of the currency, and full convertibility into gold. The Bank of England was bound to buy gold from anyone at 77s. 9d. an ounce and sell to anyone at 77s. 10½d. per ounce (this price endured for about two centuries—apart from interruptions during the Napoleonic wars and the First World War—until Britain finally left gold in 1931). At the same time, the Royal Mint was obliged to coin any gold presented to it free of charge. Hence the domestic currency automatically expanded when there was an inflow of gold and contracted when there was an outflow.

In the case of England, this stock of gold—which constituted both the country's external reserve and the reserve base of the banking system—was always very small. In the 1880s for instance it was about £20 millions (only 5 per cent or so of the volume of annual imports). Other central banks, notably the Bank of France, had a far larger gold reserve in relation to potential claims. The difference is explained by differences in financial habits—differences that persist to-day. The usual reason given is that England, as an international banker, was lending out again all its payments surplus, accumulating a large amount of long- and short-term claims on other countries, rather than hoarding its earnings in an asset that earned no income i.e. gold. As Goschen, a Chancellor of the Exchequer, succinctly put it: "England allowed foreigners to carry its gold reserve and obtained interest on it". This attitude is possible, of course, only as long as other countries have complete confidence in the currency concerned and wish to hold it—as England, and now the United States, have since discovered.

Even at that time, this small gold reserve, coupled to the rigid link with the domestic money supply, created problems. The quasi-automatic reaction to a loss of gold was to raise the discount rate. During the nineteenth century, the Bank learned how to make this "effective" in the money market by open-market operations. By vigorous increases in interest rates, the Bank was nearly always able to pull in gold from overseas and communicate an appropriate atmosphere of "crisis" to the whole business community, thus curbing the demand for credit. Yet, even then, it was necessary on occasion to borrow gold in an emergency from overseas banks (such as the Bank of France). And the violent fluctuations in interest rates certainly hampered industry. On the other hand, this economy in the use of reserves was necessary, domestically: it was only by means of most liberal lending, which created a tremendous expansion in bank deposits on the narrow gold base, that the English banking system built the "pyramid of credit" required by the growth of industrial activity. This was what Lord Keynes later called the "miracle" of "turning a stone into bread"; it was only by the substitution of a credit mechanism in place of hoarding that it was possible to avoid a deflationary pressure that would otherwise have prevented the development of modern industry. There would have been no industrial revolution without this financial revolution too.

THE TWENTIETH CENTURY

There were few big changes in the institutional structure or services of the deposit banks between the emergence of the "Big Five" (and seven smaller clearing banks, as there were then), after the First World War and the end of the 1950s. On the level of competition between banks, the main emphasis was on a rapid extension of branch networks—so that critics soon came to complain that Britain was "overbanked". There were also developments tending to restrict competition, notably the formation of the inter-bank "cartel" agreements on deposit and advances rates. It was also during this period that the deposit banks abandoned their practice of paying interest on current accounts. Many of the "conventions" which governed British banking in the generation after the Second World War were therefore fairly recent, born of the particular circumstances of the inter-war years.

There were no bank failures in the depression years between the wars. The banks were not only strong, but also, unlike many banks in other countries, had been able to keep their advances fairly liquid. So there was no need for a new legal banking code. Indeed, the tendency was rather for the deposit banks to widen and liberalize their lending policies. This was in turn a natural reaction to the relative lack of lending opportunities during the depression and the excessively liquid position of the banks.

But a big transformation of the clearing banks' balance sheet —and their whole business outlook—started in the three years 1958-60. The long period of "cheap money" (Bank rate had been unchanged at 2 per cent between 1932 and 1951, except for a pointless upward fluctuation on the outbreak of war) and the war itself had left the banks with vast swollen portfolios of liquid assets and Government securities. The ratio of advances to deposits, which had stood at about 60 per cent before the First World War, had fallen to about 30 per cent in the mid-1930s and to a low point of 17 per cent in 1945 (almost all other deposits were invested in short and long-term Government securities); by 1958 the ratio had recovered only to 30 per cent. But in no more than three years, by 1961, it had reached 47 per cent, whilst the proportion of bank deposits invested in Government securities fell from 32 per cent to 15 per cent. This transformation was due directly to the lifting of official restrictions on bank lending; these restrictions had been maintained for so long after the war because of Britain's balance-of-payments troubles and the danger of inflation.

By the early 1960s, the stage had been reached when many

bankers became concerned about a lack of deposits to support their lending opportunities, and a great debate opened as to whether the clearing banks should compete more actively for deposits by offering market rates for them. Their first reaction was to set up special subsidiaries able to offer market rates, participate in Euro-currency business, and lend on longer terms than the clearing banks themselves wished to. The banks also entered many new fields of activity, notably by taking interests in hire purchase (instalment credit) finance companies. Then they began to experiment with merchant banking business, introduced the Bank Giro, including a credit transfer system, and built up many other new services until, in 1971, they abandoned their collective agreements on deposit and lending rates and embraced open competition.

Quite suddenly in the 1960s the banks also made a big drive to popularize the "banking habit" with classes of the population previously unfamiliar with it. Previously, the banks had largely stood aside whilst the nation's "small savings" were collected by building societies, savings banks and other institutions. Nevertheless, the use of the cheque is more widespread in England than in many other countries; about 40 per cent of the total adult population now have an account with a clearing bank. Meanwhile, the banks' routine operations have been transformed by massive investment in computers. By the beginning of the 1970s, they were all moving towards the idea that they should provide, within one group, all banking services.

At the same time, the rapid growth of international money markets, and the influx of many foreign banks into London, presented the big deposit banks with a challenge. True, they had, for at least 50 years, engaged in international business (previously they had left this field to merchant banks, overseas banks and other specialists). The first move, before and after the First World War, was to set up foreign exchange departments and offer finance for foreign trade; for some time now the clearing banks have been the largest source of export finance in England. Later, some of them established representation abroad (mainly in Europe). But this side of their activity remained relatively under-developed. By 1970, they were all rethinking their international activities.

The last few years have also seen the biggest change in the institutional structure of deposit banks since 1918-22. It was started when the National Provincial and Westminster Banks announced plans for a merger with the approval of the authorities. This was quickly followed by plans to merge Barclays, Lloyds and Martins Banks to create a giant bank, which would have been far larger than any other in Britain. After referring this plan to the Monopolies Commission, the Government in 1968 vetoed the merger of Barclays and Lloyds; but Barclays was allowed to take over Martins. The reasons given for the mergers were the need to accommodate the financial needs of large industry; to compete effectively in world markets with the great American and other international banks; to rationalize branch networks and spread overhead costs. Since then the banks have been occupied with reorganizing their structures on modern lines, developing full international capabilities, and above all—still their most obvious need—developing the expertise of their staff. Salary levels, especially for trained experts that banks need, had been allowed to fall so far relatively to outside opportunities, that the banks' ability to keep up with modern developments—and give their staff an exciting career prospect—was gravely imperilled.

The most recent changes at the time of completing the revision of this guide were those flowing from the lifting of all ceilings on bank lending and the switch to the new system of credit control in 1971. The main developments in the following year were a historic rise in lending, notably in personal lending and money market business, which brought the ratio of advances to deposits up to 70 per cent; and the greater involvement of the clearing banks in credit cards, personal instalment loans, travel facilities, medium-term lending, merchant banking, insurance and investment advice. With all this went a new emphasis on "marketing" bank services, even though many observers thought that the clearing banks still had much to learn in that area.

Part II

Banking Institutions and Their Activities

DEPOSIT-TAKING INSTITUTIONS

DEPOSIT-TAKING institutions naturally comprise a wide spectrum of activities. At the heart of the system, first, are still the big deposit banks themselves; these are the largest lenders in the system, they provide the country's money transfer mechanism and their deposits constitute the main component in the money supply. Second, there are the other types of banks, namely the merchant banks, overseas banks and foreign banks; these are sometimes referred to as "wholesale banks" because they all tend to deal in large sums of money and provide services for larger customers and because, generally speaking, they do not provide "retail" banking services since they do not have large numbers of branches in England. Deposits with these banks, both in sterling and foreign currency, have been growing exceptionally fast in recent years; deposits with them of UK residents are counted as part of the money supply; and together with the deposit banks (and the new National Giro) they constitute the "banking sector" as defined by the Bank of England. Thirdly, however, there are other groups of deposit-taking institutions, notably the building societies, the hire purchase finance societies and the savings banks; these have certainly been fulfilling some "banking-type" functions, though their deposits are not officially counted as "money" and they are not part of the "banking sector".

Apart from all these deposit-taking institutions, there are naturally other financial institutions, such as the insurance companies (both life assurance and general assurance) and superannuation funds; the unit trusts and the investment trusts; the long-term capital market, and the stock exchange. These institutions are not described in this book. Table 1 shows the deposits of the major deposit-taking institutions at the end of 1971.

THE BANKING SECTOR: WHO ARE THE DEPOSITORS AND BORROWERS?

Statistics relating to the banking sector as a whole, which are compiled by the Bank of England, are most useful in highlighting not only the sources of bank deposits and the distribution of their advances, but also the shares of the various types of banks in the nation's banking business. The figures in Table 2 exclude inter-bank transactions, and so furnish a good guide to the banks' transactions with other sectors of the economy.*

The table shows that, at the end of 1971, deposits of overseas residents, equivalent to over £20,000 millions, represented over half of all deposits with the banking sector, of £38,000 millions. The table also shows the immense increase in these overseas deposits since 1965, and even 1969. This increase reflects London's role as the main centre of the Euro-dollar market. Though of course London banks have for many decades had large sterling deposits from overseas, these overseas sterling deposits have not been increasing much over recent years (apart from fluctuations) and are now only a fraction of total overseas deposits. It is also evident that most deposits of overseas residents are lent out again overseas—as the analysis of advances reveals. The growth of the Euro-dollar market has had a large impact on the institutional structure of banking in London: the table shows that the increase in overseas deposits and advances has been almost entirely concentrated in the "wholesale banks".

Of the total deposits by UK residents of about £17,000 millions in 1971, about one-third were held by corporate depositors (companies and financial institutions) and about two-thirds came from the rest of the private sector—mainly individuals, professionals, etc. On the other hand, out of the total of *advances*

*The term "deposit banks" refers to the London clearing banks, Scottish and Northern Ireland banks, and a few other banks. The term "wholesale banks" is employed to refer to the merchant banks, the overseas banks, the foreign banks in London and other money market banks. This term is not yet in widespread use in England, but there is a need for an expression that will embrace all these banks, whose operations have many points in common: and this term is intended to convey the idea that these banks deal mainly in large sums of money, and for companies rather than private individuals. In the table, the expression "Deposits" includes funds placed on current account, "time" deposits and other accounts. "Advances" include loans as well as overdrafts.

to British residents, of £12,600 millions, nearly 60 per cent was made to companies and financial institutions, nearly 20 per cent to the public sector and only 20 per cent or so to the personal and professional categories and other borrowers in the private sector. Moreover, as the table shows, advances both to the public sector and companies had been expanding over these years faster than those to other borrowers in the private sector. These figures highlight the banks' role as financial intermediaries—taking funds from individuals and lending them to industry—and the way that credit squeezes in the 1960s depressed lending to consumers. The increase in borrowing by the public sector was mainly accounted for by the local authorities (i.e. county councils, town councils, etc. in England).

Turning to the respective shares of the deposit banks and "wholesale" banks in Britain's banking business, Table 2 shows that the deposit banks still accounted for the bulk of deposits from UK residents—£13,500 millions in December, 1971 compared with £3,000 millions for the "wholesale" banks. But the share of the deposit banks had been declining quite markedly. The table shows that this has represented largely a shift in the disposition of the deposits of companies and financial institutions away from the deposit banks; indeed, in recent years corporate deposits with the "wholesale" banks have become almost as large as those with the deposit banks. The principal reason for this shift is that the "wholesale" banks have offered better interest rates than the deposit banks.

Turning to lending business, the increase in the share of the "wholesale" banks is even more striking. From 1965 to 1969 they doubled the volume of their advances to British residents and increased it another 75 per cent in the following two years, accounting for 45 per cent of all such advances by the banking sector. Again, this increase was accounted for by higher lending to companies and financial institutions and the public sector. Lending to the "Other" borrowers in the private sector—notably individuals and professional borrowers and also farmers—is still concentrated almost entirely in the hands of the deposit banks.

Looking at these figures, it is easy to understand why many bankers think that the main growth in banking in future will be in "wholesale" banking. But it is nevertheless important to remember that the deposit banks not only command massive resources, but also have developed their participation in "wholesale" business recently both either direct and through subsidiaries. It is to these banks that we turn in the next section.

But first a word about the discount market. Table 2 shows that their direct business with the general public by way of deposits and advances is small. In interpreting these figures, however, it should be remembered that they exclude inter-bank transactions—and the function of the discount market is largely to provide services to other banks. So the main part of their business is not reflected in these statistics. Secondly, the table does not show commercial bills discounted—which is a main way in which the discount market provides finance for the private sector.

Part II

A. The Deposit Banks

The deposit banks in Britain are in the midst of a revolution in their structure and activities. For a generation after the Second World War, they seemed to be on the defensive: they lost potential lending business to financial institutions outside the banking sector and to other banks. They were criticized for failing to respond to major challenges in their international and domestic business, even in their money-transfer services. The introduction of a National Giro system posed a new challenge for them. Towards the end of the 1960s, however, they began vigorously to respond to these challenges: they widened their services; some amalgamated; they started to prune their large branch networks; they developed their interests in hire purchase finance companies and their subsidiaries or affiliates previously set up to operate in the "wholesale" banking market; they took a new look at their international activities. This transformation, however, is not yet complete. Above all, it has not yet embraced a radical enough change in staffing and salary levels.

THE INSTITUTIONS

A historical outline of the development of the big deposit banks is given at the end of this section and a detailed description of their affiliates and subsidiaries is given in table 8 (parts 1, 2, 3 and 4). The big groups are the following: Barclays Group, National Westminster Group, Midland Bank Group and Lloyds Bank; there are, in addition, two independent groups based in Scotland—namely the Bank of Scotland, and the National and Commercial Banking Group. Each of these groups consists of a parent bank and various subsidiaries.

(a) The London clearing banks

The term "clearing bank" means only that the bank concerned is a member of the Committee of London Clearing Banks. Four members of this Committee are made up of the four parent banks of the groups mentioned above; that is to say, Barclays Bank Limited, National Westminster Bank Limited, Midland Bank Limited and Lloyds Bank Limited. In addition, there are two other members of the Committee: Coutts and Co., and Williams and Glyn's Bank Limited. Coutts is owned by National Westminster, but will continue to be operated as a separate bank because of its special position (it has always had a small but "high-class" clientele); Williams and Glyn's is owned by the Scottish group, the National and Commercial Banking Group (a holding company that also owns the biggest Scottish bank, the Royal Bank of Scotland). The London Clearing banks comprise the following:

Barclays Bank Limited.
Coutts and Co.
Lloyds Bank Limited.
Midland Bank Limited.
National Westminster Bank Limited.
Williams and Glyn's Bank Limited.

For many years up to the end of 1969 there had been 11 London clearing banks, with Barclays as the biggest followed by Midland, Lloyds, Westminster, National Provincial, Martins, District, Williams Deacon's, Glyn Mills, Coutts and the National Bank. But following the series of mergers in recent years, this number has been reduced to six, as on the above list; and the core of these is formed by the parent banks of the four great deposit banking groups.

These "clearing banks" account for the bulk of domestic banking activity in England.

(b) The Scottish banks

Banking in Scotland is in the hands of three banks: the Royal Bank of Scotland, the Bank of Scotland and Clydesdale Bank.

The largest of these is the Royal Bank of Scotland, which is a member of the National and Commercial Banking Group (see historical sketch on page 58).

All these banks have links with London clearing banks. Clydesdale Bank is a subsidiary of the Midland Bank. The other two are independent Scottish banks, although Lloyds Bank has a minority interest in National Commercial Banking Group, and Barclays Bank has a large minority interest in the Bank of Scotland.

The Scottish deposit banks operate on broadly the same principles and offer similar services as the English banks. The most well-known distinction of the Scottish banks is their right to issue their own bank notes. In recent times, Scottish banks have been in some respect pioneers in British deposit banking; for example, it was a Scottish bank that was the first to enter the field of hire purchase in the 1950s, a lead afterwards followed by all the big London banks.

(c) The Northern Irish Banks

Banking in Northern Ireland is mainly conducted by subsidiaries of London clearing banks (the Northern Bank is a subsidiary of the Midland, and Ulster Bank is a subsidiary of National Westminster) and by branches of banks based in the Republic.

(d) Other deposit banks

Other banks included in the Bank of England's classification of "deposit banks" are the Co-operative Bank; C. Hoare and Co.; Isle of Man Bank (a subsidiary of National Westminster); Lewis's Bank, a subsidiary of Lloyds; the Scottish Co-operative Wholesale Society Ltd Bankers; and Yorkshire Bank, which is owned jointly by Barclays, National Westminster and Lloyds.

(e) The Republic of Ireland

Banking in the Republic of Ireland will not be described in detail in this work. Suffice to say that it is controlled mainly by two banking groups: namely, the Bank of Ireland Group and the Allied Irish Banks Group. Northern Bank and Ulster Bank also have branches there.

Irish banking is currently undergoing a transformation comparable to that in English banking. Both the present banking groups emerged in the late 1960s as the result of a number of amalgamations. Both have recently recast their organizations and enlarged the services offered. In the past, many critics have complained that Ireland is "overbanked" perhaps to an even greater extent than England or Scotland.

THE ACTIVITIES OF THE DEPOSIT BANKS

The activities of the English clearing or deposit banks will be described in three sections:

1. The first section will outline the services offered by the clearing banks themselves.

2. The second section will examine the growth of the clearing banks' business from the statistics of their assets and liabilities.

3. The third section will outline, briefly, the services available from their principal subsidiaries and the growth of these subsidiaries. Increasingly these services are being presented as part and parcel of the services available from the whole "group".

1. The services of the clearing banks

The chief services of a deposit bank are, naturally, the receipt, transfer and encashment of deposits and the making of loans to customers; and its chief economic function is to provide a means whereby money (deposits) may be employed productively—whether in industry or in professional or private activity—rather than left idle. The sources of the deposits of the deposit banks, and the main distribution of their advances, by sector of the economy, have been shown in Table 2. A more detailed analysis of their advances, in February, 1972, is shown in Table 7.

In England, the deposit banks offer four principal types of banking account:

Current account. The current account opens the door to nearly all the other services offered. Accounts may be opened with very small sums of money, and the customer is provided with a cheque book and credit transfer book. Statements of the customer's account, showing a record of deposits or withdrawals, are given when he requests them, or at regular intervals (say, once a month). The customer may withdraw any amount up to the total amount deposited. The customer may borrow money, on overdraft, by arrangement with his bank manager.

The cost to the customer varies, broadly, according to the amount of work to the bank in operating the account, taking into consideration the value of the credit balance that is maintained. The larger the credit balance, for any given "turnover", the lower will be the bank charges. An official investigation in bank charges in 1967 found that over 40 per cent of the clearing banks' personal customers paid no bank charges at all, and most of the others were charged less than £4 per year. Most individuals then kept credit balances of less than £100. Naturally, banks' big corporate customers pay far higher charges corresponding to the amount of work done for them; and charges have risen fast since 1967.

Deposit account. This is a "time deposit" account—and withdrawals require, in theory, seven days' notice (although in practice modest amounts may often be withdrawn on demand). Until September, 1971, interest was paid by the bank at a rate fixed by agreement between the clearing banks, normally 2 per cent below the current level of Bank Rate; since then, banks have been forced to determine individually what deposit rate they may offer. No charges are made for operating the account.

The current account and the deposit account are by far the two most widely used of the clearing banks' accounts.

In addition, there are two subsidiary kinds of account: the *savings account,* which is intended to encourage "small savers" and on which an interest rate of 5 per cent is paid on the first £250 in the account and deposit rate thereafter (the details vary from bank to bank), and the *"budget account",* which operates also under other names and which is intended to help the regular wage or salary earner spread evenly his recurring bills. Under this scheme, the customer's total annual expenditure on items like rates, insurance, fuel and travel expenses are agreed with his banker and one-twelfth of the total amount is transferred monthly from current account to budget account, by standing orders. Cheques may be issued in payment of bills, as and when they fall due, whether or not an overdraft is created in the account.

Methods of settlement and money transfer. By far the most important method of settling debts is by *cheque* and the cheque habit is more widespread in Britain than in many other countries. In order to make cheques still more popular, the clearing banks have issued *cheque cards* which guarantee to those accepting a cheque up to a certain limit (such as shopkeepers) that it will be honoured; these cards also facilitate cash withdrawals at bank branches. Another service is the *standing order,* where a customer instructs his bank to make periodical payments of fixed amounts, and these are frequently used for regular payments, such as subscriptions to clubs, insurance premiums and so forth.

Another method of settling debts is the Bank Giro. This incorporates a *credit transfer* system; for example, a customer with many payments to make can instruct his bank to transfer to the bank accounts of his creditors the amounts due from him; he himself writes out one cheque debiting his account with the total amount. This is widely used for such matters as the payment of wages and salaries to employees. Another part of the Bank Giro system is the *direct debiting* scheme; under this, a creditor is able to claim any sums due to him direct from the debtor's bank account—with the prior approval of the debtor. This scheme is intended especially for the use of traders, and nationalized industries dealing with customers, such as gas and electricity services, as well as insurance companies, etc.

Credit cards. The first credit card scheme launched by a clearing bank itself in England was the Barclaycard offered by Barclays Bank. Unlike most other credit card schemes, it is intended for the use of housewives, and other shoppers, as well as businessmen. In mid-1972 there were about two million card holders in Britain, and it could be used at about 50,000 shops and other establishments. Barclays has co-operated in this scheme with the Bank of America, whose credit card is one of the leading credit cards in the United States.

In 1972 the other big clearing banks followed suit with a jointly owned credit card organization to launch the Access card, as a competitor to Barclaycard. Their aim of 50,000 outlets and three million Access card holders was quickly realized.

Loans and overdrafts. As already mentioned, the most popular and common form of bank borrowing in England is still by way of overdraft; under this arrangement, the customer agrees a credit limit with his banker, and is then able to draw cheques on his ordinary current account up to that limit. For large business customers, these credit limits are usually re-negotiated at regular intervals—say, every six months or every year. Branch managers are given considerable discretion to agree credit lines for their customers, whom they will interview. The overdraft has the advantage that customers borrow only as much as they need at any time, and pay interest only on the net daily overdrawn balance in their current account or accounts.

Loans for fixed periods may also be offered. Under this arrangement, the total amount of the loan is drawn and charged for from the outset of the arrangement (in the case of personal borrowers). Repayment is made by equal periodical instalments (often monthly).

Security is usually, though not necessarily, required on loans and overdrafts, and personal loans may be made unsecured.

There has been much discussion in England on the length of *period,* and on the purposes, for which the clearing banks should lend. In theory, all overdrafts are repayable on demand. In practice, many are "rolled over" from one year to the next. In theory, again, most deposit bankers are still trained in the belief that their job is to provide only short-term finance for industry, or working capital. In practice, the clearing banks provide a large volume of medium-term and longer-term finance, partly through special schemes set up with Government encouragement. For instance, there is a special scheme to help shipbuilding; and, of course, the clearing banks provide massive medium-term credit for exports. But quite apart from these special schemes, bankers have also undoubtedly broadened their conception of their business in recent years.

Other services. Amongst the other services offered by the clearing banks are the following:

Automatic cash dispensers. These are gradually being installed in the main towns and other centres. Placed in the outside wall of the bank branch or in other convenient places, they allow customers to draw out £10 in bank notes at any time of the day or night by a special electronic device.

Travellers cheques. These are naturally provided by all the clearing banks. All of them also offer *security facilities* where customers may keep documents, securities, wills, jewellery and other valuables, and *night safes,* which are convenient for shopkeepers and others who may handle large sums of money after banking hours.

In the field of personal investment, all the banks offer facilities for the sale and purchase of stocks and shares, as well as *investment advice* and *investment management.* Many of them have also entered the field of *unit trusts* and sell units through their branches. The banks also offer a full range of *executor and trustee* services, and can undertake to deal with a customer's *income tax* matters. As a further facility, cheque cards can now be used for encashment of cheques in Europe under the Eurocheque Scheme.

Finance for exports. This is a large and complicated subject, of which it is possible to give only a brief outline here. Merchant banks, overseas banks and other financial institutions are, of course, active in this field as well as the deposit banks.

The most convenient and, sometimes, still the cheapest source of export finance is the bank overdraft, granted on normal terms (as described above). The amount that the bank may be prepared to advance in this way may be increased if the exporter has a policy with the Export Credits Guarantee Department (see below), and "assigns" the proceeds of the policy to the bank. The banks normally regard this as acceptable collateral for financing trade in consumer goods (on up to six months' credit) and also for light engineering goods (on somewhat longer credit).

Sometimes it is customary in the trade or market concerned to use bills of exchange—which, for hundreds of years, have been one of the chief instruments of international trade. There are four principal techniques of providing finance that employ bills of exchange; the negotiation or discounting of documentary collections, acceptance credits, and documentary letters of credit. When a bill is "negotiated", the exporter, for a small charge, is granted additional overdraft or loan facilities to the value of the bill; where it is "discounted", it is sold to the bank at a discount. Under the acceptance credit facility, the accepting house (who are specialists in this field) or bank undertakes to "accept" bills drawn on it up to a certain agreed maximum figure, and the bills are then readily discountable, the exporter receiving cash immediately. Under the letter of credit method, the *overseas buyer* requests his local bank to have opened or confirmed in London a documentary acceptance credit in favour of the exporter; under this, the bank promises to accept bills of exchange accompanied by the shipping documents. Here again, the bills can then be easily discounted and the exporter receives his cash immediately. This is the safest arrangement of all for the seller.

Another technique is "factoring". This is a very large industry in America, and is finding its feet in England. Essentially, it offers traders insurance of their trade debts and a source of finance: the factor in effect buys the trade debts of his client, and may lend him funds against them. Many banks are now involved, directly or indirectly, in such "factoring" organizations.

Export credit insurance. All advanced countries have established special State-sponsored credit insurance agencies. In England, this is provided by the Export Credits Guarantee Department. It is the only organization in the country that insures against political as well as commercial risks. Its operations cover the insurance of export credits only (short, medium and long term). About 30 per cent of all Britain's exports are insured with the ECGD. The basic type of policy it offers is called the "Comprehensive Policy".

Comprehensive policies, offered by the ECGD, are the cheapest form of export credit insurance. Credit terms accepted for insurance vary from six months, for consumer goods and raw materials, up to five years, for the export of heavy machinery. The policies cover up to 90 per cent on commercial risks and 95 per cent on political risks. Premium rates vary greatly according to the export market involved; they average, roughly, about $\frac{1}{4}$ per cent of the value of the goods for any business up to six months' credit. The company usually has to agree to insure all its export business. The policies can be assigned to a bank, and usually are assigned; the bank may then grant finance at normal overdraft rates (2 per cent above "base rate" or whatever it may be for the particular customer).

There are several variations of this basic policy, which it is not necessary to describe here. However, it is necessary to mention the special policies developed by the ECGD in connection with special export finance schemes at favourable interest rates.

Special Export Finance Schemes. The intense international competition in exports and export finance led to the development of several special schemes under which the banks provide finance at favourable rates of interest. These schemes now cover short-term, medium-term and long-term export credits. In each case, they are tied to special guarantees given directly by the *ECGD to the banks;* this means that the banks run no risk in respect of such credits. Special refinance facilities have also been developed so that the banks do not face liquidity problems as a result of granting export credits.

In medium and long-term credits, the finance was provided by the banks at a fixed rate of $5\frac{1}{2}$ per cent until October, 1970, when it was changed, first to 7 per cent, and then to $6\frac{1}{2}$ per cent. In early 1972, the rate was fixed at 6 per cent, and the arrangement altered so that banks were assured of an average return related to market rate. A feature of the long-term finance arrangements (between five and 15 years) is that they are provided directly by the banks in the United Kingdom to the overseas buyer, who is thus able to pay the British exporter on a cash basis (the overseas buyer is required to provide 20 per cent of the purchase price, the other 80 per cent being provided by the UK banks).

Some forms of export finance are handled by subsidiaries of the deposit banks; others are handled by the parent banks.

2. *Assets and liabilities of the clearing banks, 1951-1972*

Table 4 (parts 1, 2 and 3) shows the development of the deposits, the liquid assets, the investment portfolios and the advances of the London clearing banks between 1951 and 1972.

Table 4(1) shows the distribution of deposits between current accounts, deposit accounts and other accounts (including various internal funds and accounts of the banks). "Net deposits" exclude items which are "in transit" between offices of the same bank and they also exclude cheques which are in process of being collected on other banks, as well as balances with other banks in Britain. Deposits account for about 90 per cent of the banks' total liabilities—the remainder being made up of capital, reserves, etc. As can be seen, the clearing banks have very large sums placed with them on current account—on which they do not pay interest. This reflects, partly, their unique role in the money transmission system of the country. Bank customers up and down the country—whether private individuals or companies—keep a certain amount of money in their current accounts on which they draw cheques (the average personal balance is about £150). However, "deposit accounts" have been rising rapidly as a proportion of total deposits: as customers become financially more knowledgeable, and more conscious of inflation, they are loth to leave any more than a bare minimum amount of money on current account. Since the banks pay interest on deposit accounts, this rising proportion of deposit (or time) accounts is one source of pressure on bank profits.

Table 4(2) shows the distribution of the clearing banks' liquid assets between cash (i.e. coin, notes and balances with the Bank of England), money at call and short notice, and bills (Treasury bills, commercial bills and other bills).

Throughout the period (until September, 1971) the banks were required to maintain certain minimum ratios of cash and liquid assets to gross deposits. On cash reserves, the required ratio was fixed at 8 per cent of gross deposits and the banks kept close to it; but in practice, this ratio was not important from the point of view of monetary control. More important was the liquid asset ratio, a minimum ratio of 28 per cent (30 per cent until 1963) of gross deposits. Both these ratios had their origins in the banks' need to keep a proportion of their assets in liquid form.

After September, 1971, the system was changed: the old ratios were abolished and a new "reserve assets ratio" imposed under which banks have to keep 12½ per cent of their "eligible liabilities" (mostly deposits from customers) in certain defined "reserve" assets. These assets include some that are embraced in the banks' "liquid assets" (and in the old liquid assets ratio) such as Treasury bills, commercial bills and money lent "at call" in the money market but they exclude cash held by banks (full details see page 128).

Beyond these requirements, the banks employ their deposits in two main forms; in portfolio investments (predominantly British Government securities) and in advances. These are their "risk" assets: their investment holdings contain an element of risk in that the banks may on occasion be forced to sell investments on the market (in order to sustain their reserve ratios above the $12\frac{1}{2}$ per cent minimum) at a loss; and their advances contain an element of risk through the possibility of bad debts—the default of customers. The banks' investments act as a kind of cushion; by selling investments they are able to continue to increase their advances, when there is a good demand for borrowing, whilst still sustaining their reserves. It is possible that the banks may have to sell investments at a significant loss, if prices are falling in the government securities market. Unless the authorities move in to support the market at such a time, the banks will come under growing pressure to raise their lending rates substantially and so deter potential borrowers.

Advances are the most profitable of the banks' assets; they include all credits they grant to the private sector and to nationalized industries in loans and overdrafts.

Development of assets and liabilities, 1951–72. This period should be viewed in four parts: from 1951 to 1957; from 1958 to 1960; from 1961 to 1971; and from 1971 to the present.

1. From 1951/2 to 1957 the banks were burdened with excessive liquidity and low advances: this was partly due to official restrictions on bank lending (lifted only in 1958) and partly to the fact that, owing to the liquid position of the whole economy, companies and private individuals could finance their expenditure without greatly increasing their bank borrowing. As the tables show, the proportion of advances to gross deposits was even lower in 1957 than in 1951; and the liquid assets ratio was actually higher, at 38.4 per cent (compared with 33.2 per cent).

2. The three years 1958–60 witnessed a transformation in the clearing banks' assets. This followed the ending of official restrictions on advances, and also on hire purchase credit; but bank advances would not have risen so fast if, at the same time, the economy had not been expanding. As it was, their advances (excluding advances to nationalized industries) nearly doubled in

three years—from £1,698 millions at end-1957 to £3,235 at end-1960; as a proportion of gross deposits, they rose from 25.7 per cent to 42.4 per cent. To finance this, the banks not only ran down their liquid assets (from 38.4 per cent of deposits, to 32.6 per cent) but also sold Government securities on a very substantial scale: their aggregate investment portfolios fell from about £2,000 millions to about £1,300 millions.

During 1960, however, two developments put a stop to this process; first, the economy showed signs of overheating and the Government re-imposed restrictions; secondly, the banks themselves were becoming somewhat concerned at their liquidity position and, possibly, reluctant to continue selling investments in order to expand advances.

3. The third period was from 1961 to 1971. During this period, the banks generally had a satisfactory (and very profitable) asset structure, even though their advances were kept under official restrictions for much of the time. After the economic recession of 1961 and 1962, the economy picked up again in 1963, culminating in a further boom in 1964; and despite the prolonged efforts of the Government to curb the boom, economic activity continued at a high level. Meanwhile, bank profits were also rising rapidly, due mainly to the rising trend in interest rates. Since the rate they charged on advances was then tied to Bank Rate, their earnings benefited automatically; it was not until 1968 that an effective curb was placed on domestic demand or the growth of bank deposits.

However, when the economy was finally brought firmly under control, one of the principal techniques used was *monetary policy;* this in turn put a stop to the increase in bank deposits. So the ratio of advances to deposits remained, on balance, fairly high by previous standards during these years; at the end of 1969 it was about 50 per cent. Meanwhile, the investment ratio had fallen to historically low levels, of about 10 per cent at the end of 1969—so this no longer provided any cushion against a sudden expansion of advances. And the liquidity ratio then applied was close to its minimum level (allowing for seasonal corrections).

At the same time, the clearing banks had become very conscious during this period of their loss of business to other banks, and to other financial institutions. They were providing neither enough services, nor attractive interest rates, to customers. The international banks in London, the finance companies, building societies, savings banks, even the Government itself (in the form of gilt-edged bonds) were offering better rates of interest than the clearing banks. Companies, in particular, were switching great chunks of their deposits away from the old-fashioned clearing banks, towards the progressive international banks in London, like the merchant banks and foreign banks (see Parts IIB, IIC and IID). So, as the clearing banks moved into the 1970s, they faced the possibility of a continued decline in their position in the financial system.

4. A new phase in their development began, however, in the autumn of 1971, with the introduction by the authorities of the new system of credit control. This had two main aims: first, to increase the effectiveness of official monetary policy (examined from this angle in Part IV, page 122); secondly, it was aimed at increasing competition, on equal terms, amongst all banks in Britain. Thus the new reserve asset ratio was applied to all banks. Moreover, in a radical change, the clearing banks then agreed to abandon their restrictive agreements on the rates they should offer to depositors and charge to borrowers. Thus they entered into open competition—both with each other and with other types of banks—for the deposits of the public. Immediately some banks, such as Midland and National Westminster, began to organize the money market operations under a single management and the "backdoor" subsidiaries which had been set up as a way round the restrictions (see following section) had to find new activities. The banks could now offer special rates themselves for large deposits (or indeed any deposits) rather than channel them towards their special subsidiaries as they had been doing.

This was the main reason for the huge growth of their deposits in the following months—though it was true that the underlying trend of deposit growth was also steeply upwards at that time: the money supply was growing at a record rate. Bank lending was expanding rapidly between the summer of 1971 and summer 1972 (though mostly to personal and property development borrowers rather than to industry), and money was also coming in from overseas—until, that is, the sudden speculative onslaught on sterling in June, 1972. The ample margin of spare lending capacity that had been allowed to develop during the long years of squeeze was taken up quickly. By late 1972, some banks were expecting some pressure on their liquidity (or rather their "reserve assets") and they had to put up their interest rates sharply in an effort to acquire more deposits and reserve assets.

For the longer term, there was every sign that the new climate of free competition was indeed engendering vast changes in the outlook and innovative drive of the clearing banks. Several new schemes for encouraging borrowing were unveiled; advertising campaigns were stepped up; new men were rising up through the hierarchies with a much more open-minded attitude to what they thought clearing banks should be doing. Indeed, it was becoming commonplace to hear the opinion that the job of a big bank was to provide all financial services required by customers. That this was more than an advertising line was shown by the continuing development of their related services.

3. Services and activities of the affiliates of the clearing banks

During the past 15 years, the clearing banks have acquired interests in several fields outside the traditional scope of deposit banking, mainly as a result of competition from other financial institutions. They have taken interests in existing companies. They have set up their own subsidiaries. They have joined with other banks, at home and overseas. Some details of the banks' affiliates are given in Tables 5 and 8.

Four of these areas will be mentioned, briefly, here: hire purchase; "money market" subsidiaries; merchant banking; and overseas activities. All these are connected together. Sometimes a clearing bank handles them through separate affiliates, sometimes through just one or two. Increasingly, these are all seen as part of the range of "group" services.

Hire purchase finance companies. The clearing banks entry into HP business was their first big post-war excursion into fields outside their traditional business; as so often happens, they all jumped together—and the results, to start with, were less than happy. After taking interests in hire purchase companies in 1958 in the hope of sharing in the profits of a fast-expanding business, the banks allowed them a free rein during the great consumer boom of 1959–60 and promptly ran into trouble with bad debts: a rather chastening experience.

The business of the hire purchase finance companies is mainly concentrated, even to-day, in the finance by instalment credits of motor cars and household durable goods. The true rate of interest charged by these companies is far higher than that on bank advances. Nevertheless, their total lending rose very rapidly in the late 1950s until it was about as large as the clearing banks' advances to personal and professional borrowers. In the last half of the 1960s, their business slowed down, and many of them diversified into other fields—leasing, personal loans, export credit. In 1970-72, they moved further into banking (and some became full "banks") at a time when the clearing banks, with which many of them were linked, were stepping up their own consumer-loan business. The tendency now is for the banks to bring such affiliates under their full control and management—or to sever links altogether.

"Money market" subsidiaries. These are subsidiaries which the clearing banks established during the 1960s to bid for money at market rates of interest, i.e. at the "back door" rather than at the front door of the bank itself, which could at that time offer only one, poor, deposit rate. This was often not their ostensible purpose: the banks frequently said that they were intended to conduct medium term finance, or business "outside the usual sphere of a clearing bank" or some similar phrase. But their prime reason, originally, was to offer a decent rate of interest to depositors for large sums of money, and thus win back, through this indirect means, some of the business that the parent clearing banks themselves were losing.

They soon became large operators in the money markets. They gathered large deposits quickly—most of them were only set up in the period 1964-68.

Table 6 reproduces the official statistics relating to the "Other" banks in the United Kingdom—of which the largest component is precisely these clearing bank subsidiaries. It shows a tremendous increase in their total deposits in the four years 1965–69, from about £300 millions to no less than £2,200 millions (though there were some changes in the contributors to these tables during this period); and an even more spectacular growth to 1972 when deposits with them totalled £5,000 millions. Sterling deposits from non-bank customers in Britain had grown tremendously, which suggests that many clearing banks just passed their customers on to these subsidiaries. But deposits placed by other banks and deposits in foreign currencies also rose sharply.

On the assets side, the largest component is "balances with other UK banks"—representing funds relent on the money market. These subsidiaries are also very large operators in the local authority money market (see Part III), as shown by the total of the loans to UK local authorities of £700 millions. The advent of the new credit control system meant however that the clearing banks themselves could, if they wished, offer market rates for large deposits and several of these affiliates, which had suffered greatly from the "ceilings" on lending, expanded their medium-term lending and merchant banking activities.

Merchant banking. As soon as the clearing banks decided to enter into competition, through subsidiaries, with the other banks in London, they were stimulated to search for new *outlets* for the funds attracted; at the same time, the wide range of services offered by these other banks (merchant banks, overseas banks, etc.) was one of the principal reasons for their rapid growth. Thus one thing led to another; and the clearing banks were forced, almost despite themselves, to enter, if rather gingerly, merchant banking: that means corporate finance and advice, mergers, equity participation, term loans, new issues—capital raising in all its forms. In some cases the "money market" affiliates mentioned above were adapted to this merchant banking rôle.

National Westminster has a subsidiary called County Bank that is being developed as a merchant bank. Midland has the Midland Bank Finance Corporation, a link with Samuel Montagu, the merchant bank, and Midland and International Banks Ltd., all of which conduct operations usually associated with "merchant banking". The National and Commercial Group has Williams and Glyn's, which takes in a merchant bank as well as a clearing bank. Lloyds recently formed a merchant banking division and has a majority stake in Lloyds and Bolsa International, which is busy in corporate finance as well as overseas operations. Barclays has a financial services division comprising four companies active in various aspects of merchant banking, export finance, trust services and insurance and is developing its subsidiary, Barclays (London and International), as its merchant banking arm.

Overseas activities. The clearing banks also have connections with overseas banks; both with British overseas banks and with some foreign banks (see Tables 8, 22 and Part IIC). Most of them have branches in Europe (through subsidiaries). Increasingly, these links and branches are being regarded as part of the overall banking group. Thus Barclays has Barclays Bank International (the old Barclays Bank DCO, see page 76) and Lloyds has a controlling interest in Lloyds and Bolsa.

Traditionally, the clearing banks left direct overseas representation to the British overseas banks; whilst company advice and similar services were left to the merchant banks. However, neither the overseas banks nor the merchant banks had the resources to compete effectively for the custom of the really big industrial companies; or rather, neither of them could provide a *complete service* for such companies. Only the clearing banks could do that. For many years, however, they held back from expanding their representation overseas, and from developing the other services that would be necessary. During that time, in the 1960s, the American banks—followed closely by the Japanese—forged steadily ahead. In the past few years, the clearers have made great strides quite quickly to rationalize and extend their overseas representation and develop new capabilities both in themselves and their affiliates. But they still lacked the full expertise, and all the types of staff, to act as complete international bankers to large companies.

European banking groups. It was inevitable that somebody should have the idea of creating a Europe-wide unified banking group. Unfortunately, it has proved impossible to realize so far, because of differences in legislation, ownership and residual nationalism. The nearest are, sadly for Europeans, the branches in Europe of giant American banks such as Bank of America. Yet several ambitious European banking groups have been formed as co-operative ventures by existing banks; a list is in Table 5 below. It may be seen that some have formal joint associations, others just have a working understanding; the most far reaching is that attempted by Crédit Lyonnais, Commerzbank and Banco di Roma which in 1971 began their "quasi-merger", i.e. everything short of a loss of identity. Staff are to be interchanged, procedures standardized, and common departments established. Other banks, sceptical or just interested, are watching from the sidelines.

Another co-operative venture, slightly more limited in scope but still ambitious in concept, was formed when in 1972 the banks long associated together in Midland Bank's grouping—Midland being the British partner—decided to set up a group co-ordinating company, called EBIC for short (see Table 8.3). This grouping has several joint ventures to its name in overseas territories. Both the "CCB" group and "EBIC" group have unveiled reciprocal credit schemes under which banks grant credits to customers of partner banks (abroad).

In 1972, Williams and Glyn's announced it had teamed up with another grouping of international banks to be known as Inter-Alpha banks. Yet these are the only two British banks involved in these groups that could become the great banks of the 1980s. National Westminster, Barclays and Lloyds all have associates and "close friends" it is true; all have interests round the world to a greater extent than European banks or, interestingly, Midland—which traditionally relied wholly on its correspondent network. In particular, Nat West is linked with powerful partners in the Orion group. Yet some bankers were wondering whether these three great British banks were wise to abjure a European commitment. In a fast moving situation, it would cause no surprise if some new realignment were to emerge. What was clear was that Europe's banks had to start preparing now for a situation that might obtain only in 15 years' time—effective European unity.

THE BIG DEPOSIT BANKS—HISTORICAL OUTLINE

The following sketches are based on information provided by the banks concerned (though the author remains naturally responsible for the contents).

Barclays Bank

By the last years of the nineteenth century, the number of private banks still in business was smaller than that of the joint-stock banks, and it was plain that the future lay with the "new" banks. Barclays had been operating as a private bank from Lombard Street in the City since 1736 (under various names: its origins go back even farther). It did not wish to be absorbed by any of the joint stock banks. It was in close business and family relationship with a number of other strong private banks, spread out along the East Coast of England. In 1896, 20 of these banks came together to form their own joint stock bank, Barclay & Company Limited.

The process of amalgamation and absorption gathered speed in the next few years, and Barclays, so far operating in the eastern half of England, had to extend its scope considerably if it was to keep pace with its competitors. Several more private banks were absorbed. Then, very rapidly. the bank expanded to national status. In 1916, by taking over the United Counties Bank Limited, Barclays' position in the Midlands was assured (and, still more important, a network of industrial lending outlets was acquired for the deposits built up in the rich agricultural land of Eastern England). In 1918 and 1919 other big amalgamations took place.

From 1920 onwards, with the structure of "Big Five" deposit banks established, banking development in England and Wales took a different shape. Now the pattern was one of competitive branch expansion, in which Barclays Bank participated.

In 1911, Barclays set up a Foreign Department. In 1919 it purchased a controlling interest in The British Linen Bank, a Scottish bank. This bank was sold in 1969 to the Bank of Scotland group, and Barclays now has a 35 per cent stake in the enlarged Bank of Scotland. About the same time, it gained a foothold in France, through the bank known to-day as Barclays Bank S.A. Barclays also had substantial holdings in several large overseas banks, and in 1925 these banks amalgamated as Barclays Bank (Dominion, Colonial and Overseas). In 1963 Barclays Bank Limited pioneered a new kind of overseas enterprise, in forming part of an international consortium of banks to set up the Banco del Desarrollo Economico Español (Bandesco) as a Spanish development bank. And in 1965 Barclays Bank of California was established by Barclays Bank D.C.O. and Barclays Bank Limited jointly.

Further stakes in the international field were established in 1967. In particular, Barclays joined four leading European banks and the Bank of America to form Société Financière Européenne, an organization created to solve problems arising from the member banks' international operations and help them adapt themselves to growing markets. Since then, however, Barclays has not joined the "inner ring" of SFE or the joint co-ordinating company that has resulted from that, ABECOR (Table 5). SFE is active in medium-term Eurocurrency lending.

Back in England, Barclays purchased a 25 per cent interest in United Dominions Trust in 1958, and in 1964 formed Barclays Export Finance Company Limited, offering specialized help to exporters. The stake in UDT was sold in 1972.

In 1966 the Barclays Group launched the Barclaycard (see

page 38), the first credit card to be wholly sponsored by a British bank, or indeed by any British organizations, and the first credit card in this country intended for general shopping use.

In 1968, Barclays took over Martins Bank, a London clearing bank.

The bank now (1972) has 3,000 branches in Britain; and the group employs about 80,000 people at home and abroad.

In 1971, it acquired all the capital of Barclays DCO (see page 76), in which it had previously had a majority stake, and also embarked on a full reorganization of the Barclays group. On January 1, 1972, the board of Barclays Bank Ltd. became a group board retaining its ultimate responsibilities but delegating very full powers to the boards of subsidiary companies. These companies fall into three divisions: UK division (basically responsible for the old clearing bank itself), International Division (including above all Barclays Bank International, the large overseas bank), and Financial Services Division. This latter division is essentially a grouping of related services such as merchant banking, insurance and export finance.

Lloyds Bank

Lloyds Bank originated in a partnership formed in Birmingham in 1765. The firm flourished in the growing wealth and prosperity of Birmingham and its surroundings. The crises and failures of the banking world in the early part of the nineteenth century, the growing popularity of the new joint-stock banks, and the passing of the Companies Act, 1862, determined the partners of the bank in 1865 to convert their business into a joint-stock company, namely Lloyds Banking Company Limited with a paid-up capital of £143,415. At that time, the bank had 13 offices and a staff of 50.

In the next 20 years, a network of branches was established in and around Birmingham, several the result of absorptions of other banks. In 1884, the amalgamation took place with two banks in Lombard Street, but the heart of the bank remained in Birmingham; London was regarded as no more than a special branch. In fact, it was not until 1912 that the Head Office was completely established in Lombard Street.

Over 2,400 branch banking offices now have a total of over $2\frac{1}{2}$ million current accounts; the bank presently employs over 34,000 people and the whole group about 45,000.

Like other clearing banks, Lloyds Bank has introduced computers and many ancillary services. A customer can purchase or have repaid through the bank any of the National Savings investments and can use the bank's services for conducting his stock and share transactions. For larger investors there is the Investment Management Service.

Among other services are cheque cards, executorship and trusteeship services, management of pension funds, and a fully computerized company registration service. Lloyds Bank operates its own Unit Trusts, units of which can be bought and sold over any branch counter.

An important step was the formation of Lloyds Associated Banking Company to operate in the money markets and undertake medium-term lending.

The overseas department of the bank, with its main office in London and branches in provincial centres, handles a massive volume of foreign business. An international banking service includes usual facilities for the finance of overseas trade, for the transfer of payments to and from countries overseas, and for dealing in foreign exchange.

Lloyds and Bolsa International, in which Lloyds Bank has a majority interest, is regarded as the international banking arm of Lloyds group. LBI was formed in 1971 from the merger of Bank of London and South America—an old-established and very active overseas bank (see page 78)—with Lloyds Bank Europe, a subsidiary of Lloyds operating some branches on the continent.

Lloyds Bank also has a shareholding in National and Grindlays, another British overseas bank with branches in East Africa, the Middle East, India and the Far East; and it owns the National Bank of New Zealand.

Midland Bank

Midland Bank was founded in Birmingham in 1836 by Charles Geach, a Cornishman from St. Austell who was working as a clerk in the Birmingham branch of the Bank of England. He was dissatisfied with his salary and with his prospects of promotion, and evidently decided that the only way to improve these was to start a bank of his own—the Birmingham and Midland Bank. The early years were not easy, particularly those between 1840 and 1870 when there were many bank failures; but the Birmingham and Midland survived and prospered. The bank purchased several small banks in the mid-nineteenth century, but it was not until the last decade of the nineteenth century that the process of amalgamations began to gather speed. The bank took over banks in Coventry, Derby and Leeds, and in 1891 felt strong enough to venture into London, by amalgamating with a London bank. Further mergers took place in the following years culminating in the merger in 1918 with the Joint Stock Bank.

Since then, Midland has acquired two more affiliates. These are Clydesdale Bank (a Scottish bank) and Northern Bank which has branches in Eire and in Northern Ireland. A large number of branches have been opened to fill in gaps in the bank's branch network throughout the United Kingdom.

Since the beginning of the century, the Midland has extended its business into fields other than straightforward banking. In 1909 the Executor and Trustee Company was formed, and a few years later the first decisive step into overseas business was taken. Apart from the main overseas branch in London with 1,300 staff, there are now several overseas branches in provincial towns, and over 20,000 banking correspondents and agents all over the globe. In 1958 the Midland entered the field of hire-purchase by purchasing, jointly with the Clydesdale Bank, the capital of Forward Trust Limited, an instalment finance company based in Birmingham. To strengthen its international activities in 1965, the Midland entered into a loose link-up with three European banks, the Amsterdam-Rotterdam Bank, the Deutsche Bank and the Banque de la Société Générale de Belgiquc (now known as Société Générale de Banque). This agreement, known as the European Advisory Committee (EAC), did not involve any exchanging of capital, but created a means by which the four banks could co-operate more fully.

Also in 1965 the Midland announced the creation of a new bank, Midland and International Banks Limited (MAIBL). This was created jointly by Midland Bank, The Commercial Bank of Australia, the Standard Bank (South Africa) and the Toronto-Dominion Bank, and its object is to provide worldwide financing in sterling or foreign currencies.

In 1970, the European Advisory Committee was formalised by the creation of European Banks International Company (EBIC). The objects of EBIC (now known as European Banks International) are to co-ordinate and promote the common activities and interests of the participating banks. EBIC was enlarged in 1971 when Société Générale of France and Creditanstalt-Bankverein of Austria became members.

Midland and its European partners have participated in a

number of joint ventures, mostly concerned with medium term lending. These include Banque Européenne de Crédit à Moyen Terme, in Brussels; European-American Banks in the USA, and Euro Pacific Finance Corporation in Melbourne. In addition, Midland Bank is a member of multi-national investment companies in South America, Africa and Asia. It also has representative offices in Brussels, Zurich, Djakarta, Toronto and Johannesburg. The Brussels and Zurich offices are purely Midland Bank operations. The others are maintained jointly by the six EBIC partners.

Midland Bank Finance Corporation Limited, (MBFC) formed in 1967, accepts sterling deposits and provides finance for development expenditure, with a special interest in major capital projects. A range of instalment credit facilities is provided by MBFC's wholly owned subsidiary, Forward Trust Limited.

MBFC further extended its interests to provide a greater range of financial services. Midland Montagu Industrial Finance Limited, was formed, in association with Samuel Montagu and Co. Limited, merchant bankers, to provide equity capital and management assistance to private companies with first-class growth potential. Midland Bank has a major shareholding in Montagu Trust Limited, which owns Samuel Montagu and Co. Limited.

To provide full factoring and invoice discounting services, MBFC and First National City Bank set up Midland—Citibank Factors Limited in 1970. Also, MBFC is a member of a consortium, Airlease International, which is concerned with substantial leasing operations involving aircraft and ships.

The new credit control arrangements which came into being in October, 1971 have resulted in considerable changes in the Midland and other banks. The bank is now able to offer medium-term loans and can accept deposits for varying periods from call to five years fixed. Additionally, the banks were enabled to revitalize their personal lending schemes. The Midland has also introduced a revolving credit scheme, with its Personal Credit Plan.

The most major recent development is that Midland Bank, together with Trust Houses Forte and the Automobile Association have acquired Thos. Cook and Sons, the travel agency.

Midland Bank has some 2,700 branches in England and Wales, and the Midland Bank Group as a whole employs some 50,000 people.

National Westminster Bank

The National Westminster Bank was formed in 1968 to effect the merger between three large banks—the Westminster Bank, the National Provincial Bank, and the District Bank. National Westminster Bank has traded under its own name since January 1, 1970, when the three component banks were amalgamated and lost their separate identities. Each of these three banks can trace its history to the early days of joint-stock banking in England in the 1820s and 1830s.

The history of the Westminster Bank is bound up, to a very large extent, with that of its three main constituent banks, the London and Westminster Bank, which opened for business in London in 1834, the London and County Bank, established in Southwark in 1836, and Parr's Bank, which commenced business in 1782 as a private bank. The London and Westminster was the first joint-stock bank to be established in London.

As a result of pressure by the founders of the London and Westminster Bank on Parliament, a clause was inserted in the Bank Charter Renewal Act of 1833, declaring that it was legal for a joint stock bank to carry on the business of banking in London, provided that it did not issue notes. The London and Westminster confined its operations to the Metropolitan area. By 1880, the year in which it was registered as a limited liability company, it had only seven branches. In 1909, the London and Westminster amalgamated with the London and County Bank. The merger was followed in 1918 by a second important amalgamation, this time with Parr's Bank. In 1923, the title of Westminster Bank Limited was adopted.

In the international field, the year 1921 saw the opening of the office of the bank's New York representative. More recently the bank, through Westminster Foreign Bank, joined with the Banco de Vizcaya and a number of other banks to establish the Banco do Financiacion Industrial, whose object is the provision of medium and long-term finance to Spanish industry. Another interesting Spanish venture was the participation by Westminster Foreign Bank in 1965 in the establishment of the important investment company, Financiera Española de Inversiones S.A. (Finsa). In 1965, too, the bank, in partnership with banking friends, including the Royal Bank of Canada, established the RoyWest Banking Corporation, with its Head Office in Nassau,

The National Provincial Bank was founded in 1833 by a timber merchant called Thomas Joplin, who was one of the most fervent critics of the banking system of his day—a system characterized by a multiplicity of small private banks. The first branch was opened at Gloucester on January 1, 1834, and by the end of that year, eleven branches had been established. The practice was to take over, wherever possible, an existing well-established local bank with its own note issue.

Early in its history, the claims of Joplin for joint-stock banking were fully tested by the experience of the National Provincial, notably in 1857 when the American crisis burst upon the country and several investment houses began to topple, and again in 1866 with the failure of Overend Gurney and Co. In that year, the National Provincial Bank decided to establish itself in London. It had by this time 122 branches in the country and was strong enough to compete with the large and well-established metropolitan banks. Other banks were taken over in following years.

In 1958, the National Provincial extended its interests into the field of hire-purchase finance by acquiring the whole of the ordinary share capital of North Central Finance.

National Westminster Bank now has in excess of 3,400 branches in England and Wales, open daily, and it has over 58,000 employees.

Internationally, it is linked with other very large banks (see Table 8.2) in joint ownership of the Orion Banking Group in London, which is mainly a vehicle for providing large-scale finance for multinational corporations. Many of its international operations are conducted through International Westminster Bank (formerly Westminster Foreign Bank), especially in Europe where it has branches and subsidiaries. County Bank is gradually being built up as a proper "merchant bank", whilst HP/instalment credit and similar facilities are centred on a subsidiary now known as Lombard North Central. Other interests, though by no means all, are shown in Table 8.2.

Altogether, the difficulties presented by the merger had been largely overcome by 1972 and its benefits in modernizing the organization, structure and style of the bank were becoming steadily more apparent.

National and Commercial Banking Group

This group owns two banks—one is Scotland and one in England; namely, the Royal Bank of Scotland and Williams and Glyn's Bank.

1. The Royal Bank of Scotland. Established by Royal Charter in 1727, it owes its origin to the compensation money—known as the Equivalent—paid to Scotland under the terms of the Act of Union of 1707, settlement of which was made partly by way of debentures of the new Government. Holders of these debentures decided to extend their activities to banking and were granted a Royal Charter to form a new corporation to be known as The Royal Bank of Scotland.

Apart from expanding its branch system in Scotland to meet the demand for local banking facilities, the bank absorbed between the two world wars the old London private banking houses of Messrs. Drummond, acquired the business of the Western Branch of the Bank of England and the entire capitals of Williams Deacon's Bank Limited and Glyn, Mills and Co.

In February, 1968, the announcement was made of the proposal to merge with the National Commercial Bank of Scotland Limited. The capital of the two banks has since been combined in a holding company called National and Commercial Banking Group Limited and in April, 1969 these two banks merged with the title, The Royal Bank of Scotland Limited.

(The National Commercial Bank of Scotland Limited was formed in 1959 by the merger of The Commercial Bank of Scotland Limited and The National Bank of Scotland Limited through both of which had a history dating back to the early nineteenth century. Both received a Royal Charter of Incorporation in 1831.)

With over 700 branches, the Royal Bank of Scotland now offers a full banking service in Scotland and London. The bank is closely associated with Lloyds and Scottish Finance Limited, a leading hire purchase company, and National Commercial and Glyns Limited, a merchant bank.

2. Williams and Glyn's Bank. This bank emerged in 1970 from the amalgamation of three former London clearing banks: Williams Deacon's Bank, Glyn, Mills and Co. and the National Bank. The bank has recently entered factoring, leasing and insurance advisory services and is concentrating on merchant banking business in a subsidiary called Williams, Glyn and Co.

It has an interest in a medium-term bank, United International Bank, and is in the Inter-Alpha group.

The Bank of Scotland

Scotland's oldest banking institution, the Bank of Scotland, was established in 1695, at a time when Scotland was just emerging from long years of civil strife and from the shock caused by the Massacre of Glencoe. The country was poor and undeveloped and was suffering from the effects of foreign wars as well as of unrest at home. The population was only about a million, and Scotland's entire annual revenue barely amounted to £100,000. The practice of banking, even in its most elementary form, could hardly be said to exist. But the pioneer spirit was abroad in the land, and, despite so unpromising a background, the scheme of establishing a Scottish bank took shape.

Just as the Bank of England owed its formation in 1694 to the enterprise of a Scotsman, William Paterson, so an Englishman, John Holland (a merchant in the City of London) was largely associated with the foundation of the Bank of Scotland. The original capital was only £100,000 sterling, with £10,000 paid up. The bank began purely as a money-lending and note-issuing institution. The bank's business was unpleasantly affected by the rebellions in support of the Stuarts of 1715 and 1745. When the 1715 trouble broke out, the whole of the specie was withdrawn, the directors privately encouraging the public's excited demand for their money lest it should fall into the insurgents' hands.

The appearance of Prince Charlie and his Highland Army in Edinburgh in 1745 had again the effect of drying up the business of the bank. But with the establishment of more settled times, the bank's business progressed. Trade and commerce were retarded by the war with the American Colonies between 1772 and 1783, but a marked revival followed the peace; Scotland and its banking institutions benefited. Efforts by the Bank of Scotland to establish a branch system, fruitless in its earlier years, were at last successful in the late part of the eighteenth century.

While maintaining its own independence throughout its long history, the bank has made important absorptions in the past 80 years and entered many new lines of business.

In 1970, it took over the British Linen Bank and has recently formed new international connections: for example, it has an interest in Banque Worms of Paris.

Part II

B. The Merchant Banks

The title "merchant bank" is difficult to define: it has no judicial significance, but is in widespread use. Some of the smaller banks that would lay claim to this name bear little resemblance to one of the larger accepting houses. The work conducted by these merchant banks varies greatly from one bank to another. Seventeen of these are gathered together in the exclusive Accepting Houses Committee, though membership of that body carries less significance than it once did. Others are members of the Issuing Houses Association. They are all small banks compared with the clearers, and have few if any branch offices—though some have outposts in the provinces and most have strong overseas connections. The number of staff employed ranges from about 50 to about 1,000 or so in a large merchant bank such as Hill Samuel, Hambros or Kleinwort Benson. They pride themselves on flexibility and speed of decision-taking, though these qualities have been difficult to retain into an age where a bank has to be quite big to be of much use to big companies. At the end of 1972, the Bank of England opened wide the doors to mergers between merchant banks and clearing banks or other European banks, so many of them may be taken over in the next few years. Even now there is no longer much that distinguishes them as a group from other banks in London except for their "names", status and connections.

Very broadly, these banks provide specialist services for industry and commerce. But the business of merchant banks is changing rapidly. Twelve years ago, foreign issues—one of the traditional fields of business—had almost withered away. It has since seen a resurgence in the form of Euro-bond issues, in which several of the London houses are involved. Another traditional area of business, arranging trade finance by means of acceptance

Credits, also recovered during the 1960s. But it is in fields of business unheard of a dozen years ago—term lending, new types of advisory work, the new money markets, leasing, factoring and the like—that many banks expect most of their future growth. Despite this variety it is, however, possible to set down four broad fields of business common to all the major merchant banks. These are described below. A fifth section looks at other areas of business in which some of the banks are participating.

Virtually all these services they provide for British industry, in marked contrast to the last century.

1. MAKING NEW CAPITAL ISSUES, AND COMPANY SERVICES

A fundamental role of the merchant banks to-day is raising capital for British industry. This is done in the main by making issues of shares and bonds on the London Stock Exchange. The essence of the merchant banks' role in making such issues is to act as sponsors and underwriters rather than as sources of finance.

A good description of the issuing procedure comes from the Radcliffe Report*:

> "The normal procedure is for the form of the issue to be discussed first with the client who wants to raise the money. The broker to issue is then called in and the form of the issue, its likely reaction on the market, and the price at which it is to be made, are discussed, frequently in a tripartite meeting. The issuing house may at about the same time take soundings of some of the big insurance companies which will later be asked to underwrite the issue. More or less simultaneously with the signing of the main underwriting contract, arrangements are made, usually through the broker to the issue, for the sub-underwriting of most or all of the issue by a wide circle of institutional investors... The sub-underwriters bind themselves, for a commission, to subscribe for stock if the public subscription falls short of the total issue. The issuing house, however, retains, as main underwriter, the ultimate responsibility for finding the money promised..."

Of the issues themselves, the split is fairly even between loans

* Committee on the Working of the Monetary System: Report, Cmnd. 827, HMSO, London, 1959.

and equity capital. In 1971, total ordinary share issues raised £272 millions against £273 millions of fixed interest bonds, but in the first half of 1972 there was a great surge of new equity issues. In most previous years in the previous decade, more bonds were issued than shares. The preference for one or the other depends both on sentiment towards equities, and on current tax legislation. For example, devaluation of sterling in November, 1967, encouraged an equity boom in 1968. By contrast, the introduction of corporation profits tax and capital gains tax two years earlier had encouraged fixed interest securities.

Other issues are made by leading stockbrokers. While it is probably fair to say that a stockbroker will make an issue more cheaply than a merchant bank (in that its fee would be lower), any of the leading merchant banks would claim that they were able to offer a service better tailored to the needs of each individual firm. The whole service of corporate financial advice has bounded ahead in the last decade—not only how to raise money, but also advice on mergers and take-overs, company reconstruction, etc.

The smaller companies are perhaps not so well provided. The so-called Macmillan "gap"—where companies too small to go public and too large to rely on local branch bank funds found it hard to raise capital—was highlighted in 1931. The Industrial and Commercial Finance Corporation, set up in 1945, is one such body which provides finance for the smaller companies.

2. CARRYING OUT FOREIGN BUSINESS

One of the most remarkable features of banking business in London in the past 12 years has been the growth of foreign business of the merchant banks and other wholesale banks. The main reason is, of course, the bounding Euro-dollar market. In the late 1950s, UK merchant banks were forced by restrictions on the use of sterling to finance overseas trade between third countries to discover a new source of finance; they were quick to realize the implications of the Euro-dollar. To start with, they used it to supplement sterling as a means of trade finance. Then they started to provide medium-term credits to international business, and arrange Euro-bond issues. Thus their old-established foreign security business reappeared in a new form. In recent years, both N. M. Rothschild and S. G. Warburg have been among the top Euro-bond issuing houses.

The provision of foreign loans, short or long term; trade

credit and the arrangement of medium or long-term export credit; advising UK companies on overseas expansion or foreign companies on opportunities in Britain; finding suitable partners and putting through the deal; advising international corporations on the distribution of their liquid funds—these would all be examples of "foreign" business that merchant banks undertake; though today other banks in London can undertake them too.

3. INVESTMENT PORTFOLIO MANAGEMENT

The merchant banks all recognize the growing demand for professional investment management services and offer such advice. Some, such as Robert Fleming, have specialized in this business. In general, five main types of fund are managed: private individuals' portfolios (in order to accept the management of a private portfolio it would have to be worth at least £50,000 or £100,000); pension funds of companies; investment trusts; and two recent additions—unit trusts and various "offshore" funds. The total volume of funds managed by a merchant bank might run into several hundred million pounds up to £1,500 millions or so.

In managing unit trusts, merchant banks have on occasion teamed up with deposit banks, whose branch networks make ideal retail outlets for such trusts. They have also joined with life assurance companies in providing unit-linked life assurance.

Offshore funds are funds based in one of the "tax havens": Bermuda, Bahamas, Channel Islands, Luxembourg, etc. This also forms a growing field of business. The advantage of these "tax havens" funds to this type of investor is that there are few, if any, restrictions on capital movements, and that dividends can be paid free of withholding tax. Investors could come from any country in the world (sometimes through numbered bank accounts) while funds may similarly be invested in every country. Several of the London merchant banks have New York offices, a part of whose work is to manage such funds.

4. COMMERCIAL BANKING

Just as some merchant banks have been keen to build up their services to companies—to make bigger earnings from advisory fees—others have needed or sought primarily to enlarge their deposit base, to give them greater lending capacity. All of them do such commercial banking business—taking large-scale deposits, both from business clients and from other banks, issuing certificates of deposit, placing funds in the various fixed-interest markets, and lending money to customers. There is also a trend towards term lending, which like many other factors is tending to involve them more closely in the business of their customers.

Acceptance business.

This is the traditional business of the merchant banks : the system that they developed during the last century to finance trade. The service consists essentially of adding the name and reputation of the bank to a bill of exchange. The cost to the trader of bill finance consists of the discount on the bill, a commission to the accepting bank, and stamp duty.

This form of business suffered a considerable decline during the 1930s and the war years. It only grew slowly in the 1950s with the increasing use of straight bank borrowing to finance trade. It has, however, recovered substantially during the last decade thanks, in the main, to controls on other bank lending. For much of this period, the clearing banks were subject to ceilings on their level of advances. Though ultimately controls were also extended to bill business, it is fair to say that the same degree of rigour was not applied. As a result, acceptances of the accepting houses rose from £130 millions at the end of 1959 to £310 millions in September, 1969; in 1972 they were about £350 millions.

5. OTHER BUSINESS

In addition to the main areas of business outlined above, most merchant banks have in the past 10 years or so been entering a number of completely new fields.

(a) Company development

Since the war, some merchant banks have made a business out of injecting their own capital into a company by taking an interest in its equity. The form that such investments take varies greatly. Sometimes it is little more than taking a trade investment in a favoured client. In this case, the bank would play no part in the management of the firm. At other times, the aim of the merchant bank is to build up the size of a company with the view either to floating it as a public company or to selling it off to a larger group. On other occasions a bank might mount a rescue operation for a firm that is in difficulties.

This form of investment banking is a relatively new departure for the accepting houses. Not all undertake it on any scale. It has, however, accounted for the rapid growth of several of the newer merchant banks and is narrowing down the differences between merchant banking and the work of industrial or commercial holding companies.

The proportion of British industry owned by merchant banks in this way remains very small. While many of the long-established merchant banks—the members of the Accepting Houses Committee—have substantial investments in allied financial institutions (like insurance, or bullion dealing) most of the *industrial* investments they hold are really incidental to their business of providing corporate advice. And do they have the industrial or managerial "know-how" for a closer involvement?

However, the type of investment bank which has grown up since the last war—for example, Slater Walker, which became a bank in January, 1970—often regards the taking of equity interests in industrial companies as its main business. These banks' work is in some ways much closer to that of a French "banque d'affaires".

(b) Leasing

Industry also uses the leasing services of the merchant banks: ships, aircraft and computers being the main items leased. The bank (usually through a subsidiary) buys the goods, then lets them out on contract.

(c) Factoring

Several merchant banks now have interests in factoring companies. Reduced to its simplest form, a factoring company undertakes to pay a client's invoices (immediately, if the client wishes —or before the date they would normally have been settled). It then recovers the full amount from the debtor. The customer therefore gains both insurance for its trade debts and working capital.

(d) Other types of business

In addition to the above, a number of merchant banks carry out other activities. Some trade in the "secondary market" in Eurobonds; some make a feature of tax or estate matters; others focus on particular industries; a few are involved in promissory note placements, a market in Euro-currency medium-term paper.

Finally, virtually all the major merchant banks have some interests in allied fields: insurance broking, commodity broking, or bullion dealing. And these are only examples.

THE LONDON GOLD MARKET

Gold has been dealt in London for centuries, but the present form of the market and its system of "fixing" is quite recent. The first meeting of the "fixing" was in the offices of Rothschild in 1919 where it still takes place.

There are five members of the market: Mocatta and Goldsmid, Sharps Pixley and Co., N. M. Rothschild and Son, Johnson Matthey and Co., and Samuel Montagu and Co.

The procedure at the "fixing", which takes place twice a day, is described by the houses as follows:

> "An opening price is suggested and all declare their intentions —as buyers, sellers or without interest at that price. When there are both buyers and sellers, each member declares the amount of his interest and if a balance is achieved, that price is the fixed or published price. Should demands from buyers exceed selling, then higher prices are tried until either a balance is reached or the buyers are willing to share the gold offered in proportion to their demands."*

But though the fixing system is the most notable feature of the London gold market, by no means all the business is done at either of the fixings. Throughout the day, deals are conducted by telephone and telex with customers in Britain and abroad at prices close to the fixing price. It is likely that a much larger proportion of the total gold trading is done in this way than at the fixing itself.

At the beginning of the Second World War, the market was closed. It was not reopened until March, 1954. From then until March, 1968, it was by far the largest gold market in the world, with both the world's largest producer of gold, South Africa, selling its output through London and, from 1960, the "gold pool" working through it. (The gold pool was the club of central banks which stabilized the free market price of gold close to the then official price of $35 per fine ounce, from 1960 to 1968.)

* *The London Gold Market,* 1969, published by the members of the London Gold Market.

Thereafter, its operations were to some extent curtailed. Most estimates in mid-1972 put its business as well below that of Zurich, its only real rival.

HOW THE MERCHANT BANKS' BUSINESS HAS GROWN

The development of the liabilities and assets of the members of the Accepting Houses Association are shown in Table 11. This may be compared with Tables 12, 13, 14, 15 and 16.

It should be said at the beginning that a large part of the business of these banks does not show up in the statistics of their assets and liabilities. Historically, their profits derived mainly from acceptance commissions. The large merchant banks are also the main source of financial advice to Britain's large industrial and commercial companies—for which services they receive fees.

Nevertheless, their deposit banking activities and their operations in the money markets are extensive, as the table shows. Their deposits from UK residents (not banks) totalled about £1,120 millions in 1972, which was more than that of any other group of non-clearing banks (except, confusingly, the subsidiaries of the clearers themselves!). Their deposits from other UK banks have also increased sharply—reflecting the growth in the inter-bank market in sterling deposits; most of these deposits are re-lent again, to other banks in the market (as shown by the figure "balances with other banks"). Accepting houses are in a good position to profit by such activity because of the strength of their "names". The same applies to their activity in Euro-currency business—shown in the big increase in the deposits from overseas residents denominated in foreign currencies.

Turning to the assets side, it can be seen that, as home-based banks they keep a high proportion of sterling deposits in liquid form (whereas many of the foreign banks in London lend their entire deposits from non-bank residents in the UK to customers in the UK, except what they have to set aside as reserve assets, since they can rely on other sources for their liquidity). But, after many years of high liquidity (i.e. spare lending capacity), sterling advances to UK companies rose rapidly when the credit restrictions were relaxed in 1971. Nevertheless, they lagged increasingly behind some of their competitors, such as the American banks.

The remainder of the accepting houses' resources were employed in the money markets (and a small part in British Government securities). The table shows that they maintain large balances with other UK banks, and also lend on a very large scale to UK local authorities. Part of the balances with other UK banks are in foreign currencies, whilst a large proportion of the Euro-dollars deposited with them in London is lent out again to overseas residents. They have been pioneers in the development of Euro-dollar business.

TEN LEADING MERCHANT BANKS—A BRIEF ACCOUNT

The following is a list of 10 of the important merchant banks. Some idea of their size is given by the latest available balance sheet figures for deposits, but because of the varied nature of their business, it is by no means the only one.

Baring Brothers and Company

(Deposits, December 31, 1971, £143 millions)

Barings is the oldest of the City merchant banks: Barings was founded as John and Francis Baring in 1763; the name was changed to the present form in 1806, and it became a limited company in 1891. The bank played a substantial part in the development of British merchant banking during the nineteenth century when, together with Hambros and Rothschilds, it formed the leading group of merchant banks. During that time, the bank had to withstand several crises, gravest of which was the "Baring Crisis" of 1890. To-day it remains a major merchant bank offering a full range of services to national and international companies.

Hambros Bank

(Deposits, March 31, 1971, £517 millions)

Perhaps the most famous of all the London merchant banks, Hambros Bank is probably still on some measurements the largest; it was founded in 1839 as C. J. Hambros. It became a public quoted company in 1936, but Hambros family interests have substantial holdings through Hambro Trust. It has long had special connections with Scandinavia and with shipping finance, which it retains. But now it is heavily involved in many other newer areas of merchant banking: providing company services and investment advice, computer and aircraft leasing, factoring, as well as making industrial and other investments on its own account.

Amongst its subsidiaries is Mocatta and Goldsmid, one of the five bullion dealers or brokers which fix the gold price on the

London Market. It also has widespread international connections, with several representative offices. It opened a New York subsidiary, Hambro American in 1968, and in partnership with three American banks, launched a Eurocurrency lending bank, Western American Bank in London in the same year; the latter bank specializes in making medium-term loans (usually in dollars) to international companies.

Hill Samuel & Company

(Deposits, March 31, 1971, £460 millions)

Formed following the merger in 1965 between M. Samuel and Philip Hill Higginson Erlangers (itself the result of a merger between Philip Hill and Partners, Higginson and Company, and Erlangers). Philip Hill was built up after the Second World War as a West End house; it was one of the first banks to see the great new opportunities in the provision of finance and advice for UK industry, and it specialized in new issues and company mergers. M. Samuel, which dates back to 1831, was one of the City's most venerable merchant banks, with well-established acceptance business. Measured on deposits, Hill Samuel is one of the largest of the merchant banks and particularly active in company financial services. To further these, it has established provincial offices in Manchester, Cardiff, Birmingham and Bristol. It also has widespread representation overseas, mainly through subsidiaries.

Among its subsidiary companies are Lambert Brothers, involved in shipbroking and chartering, and Noble Lowndes, an industrial and financial investment group.

Kleinwort, Benson

(Deposits, December 31, 1970, £414 millions)

Founded in 1830 as Kleinwort Sons, merged with Robert Benson Lonsdale in 1962. Its parent company, Kleinwort, Benson, Lonsdale has been publicly quoted since 1961.

To-day, like Hill Samuel, it is particularly strong in its company services—arranging new issues and take-overs, and offering corporate financial advice. It is also involved in the M. & G. group of unit trusts in which it has an interest, the leasing of aircraft, factory equipment, etc., and portfolio management, as well as traditional acceptance business. The group owns Sharps Pixley and Company, bullion dealers, and operates subsidiary companies in Brussels, Geneva, the Channel Islands, and the United States.

Lazard Brothers

(Deposits, December 31, 1971, £221 millions)

Controlled since the 1930s by S. Pearson and Son, the industrial holding group, a quoted company in turn controlled by Lord Cowdray's family interests. Lazards was formed in 1877, and bought Edward de Stein in 1960. It has made a notable range of company issues in the last few years—its customers include some of the largest in the country. There is not, at present, a shareholding connection with either Lazard Freres et Cie of Paris or Lazard Freres and Co. of New York. The three banks do, however, have a joint subsidiary, Lazard S.A. in Paris.

Morgan Grenfell

(Deposits, December 31, 1971, £183 millions)

Morgan Grenfell was formed in 1838 as George Peabody. Its name was changed to J. S. Morgan in 1864 and to the present name in 1910. It has long had strong American connections; 31 per cent of its capital is held by Morgan Guaranty Trust Co. of New York. The American connection has been reflected in the bank's business: it has been notable in making new issues for subsidiaries of US companies in Britain. It has also a good range of British industrial clients. Internationally, it has wide interests including a stake in the Paris Bank, Morgan et Cie, and offices in Rome and Munich.

Samuel Montagu

(Deposits of parent company, end March, 1971, £302 millions)

Formed in 1853 as Samuel and Montagu. Its parent company, Montagu Trust, has been quoted on the London stock exchange since 1963. It is one of the few merchant banks which has a direct connection with a domestic deposit bank: it is $33\frac{1}{3}$ per cent owned by Midland Bank. Samuel Montagu carries out the normal range of merchant services with emphasis on foreign currency dealing, company financial advice and on portfolio management. It also is involved in unit trusts and notably in bullion dealings, and has interests in Switzerland (Guyerzeller Zurmont Bank), France (a 20 per cent share of Credit Vendome, of Paris) and Australia (27 per cent of Capel Corporation). The group has substantial interests in insurance broking in Britain and abroad. It provides venture capital through Midland Montagu Industrial Finance.

N. M. Rothschild and Sons
(Deposits, March 31, 1971, £125 millions)

One of the oldest of London's merchant banks—it was formed by Nathan Rothschild in 1804. The corporate partner is Rothschild Continuation. Besides offering a full range of merchant banking services, Rothschild is linked with a number of American banks through Rothschild Intercontinental, a London-based bank specializing in Eurocurrency business. It also is involved in Euro-bond issuing, and its international interests include subsidiaries in Australia and New York.

J. Henry Schroder Wagg and Company
(Deposits of group, end December, 1971, £419 millions)

Founded 1804 as J. Henry Schroder, it merged with Helbert Wagg in 1962. Together with H. Henry Schroder Banking Corporation (of New York) it is the main subsidiary of Schroders Limited, a holding company controlled by the Schroder family. Other subsidiary or associated companies operate in Switzerland, Australia, Republic of Ireland, Lebanon and Spain. It has offices in Paris, Frankfurt, Argentina and Brazil, and a branch in Nassau.

S. G. Warburg
(Deposits, end March, 1972. £167 millions)

Though formally founded in 1864 as Seligman Bros, which merged with Warburgs in 1957, this is, in effect, a post-war bank. It is controlled by Mercury Securities, the financial and service industry holding group of Sir Siegmund Warburg. Besides the usual banking services, Warburgs is one of the leading banks in Europe in making Euro-bond issues. It has international interests in Frankfurt, Hamburg, New York, Zurich and Basle.

In 1973 it formed a close connection with Paribas, the French "banque d'affaires".

Part II

C. The British Overseas Banks

The principal British "overseas" banks—that is to say, banks based in London but operating extensively overseas—are Barclays Bank International, Standard and Chartered Bank, Lloyds and Bolsa International, and National and Grindlays Bank. To this list has usually been added the Hongkong and Shanghai Banking Corporation, though this bank is registered in and managed from Hong Kong. These banks are in a process of rapid structural change and have yet to find their modern role in British international banking. They are large, but perhaps not large enough to be fully viable as modern independent international banks on a world-wide scale, and their staff often still lacks the range of skills and resources possessed by, for example, the big US banks.

The main affiliates and branch networks of these banks are listed below. Several of them have links to the big deposit banks: Barclays Bank International is indeed an integral part of the Barclays Group; Lloyds Bank has a majority interest in Lloyds and Bolsa International and a considerable interest in National and Grindlays Bank. These links between British banks have been tightened in recent years, and one way forward would be for each of them (except perhaps the Hongkong Bank) to come under the wing of a great deposit bank. Two US banks have also taken minority interests in overseas banks: namely First National City Bank in National and Grindlays, and Chase Manhattan in the Standard-Chartered Bank group (this, however, is a small interest). The ready-made overseas branch networks run by such UK banks are obviously tempting to US banks wishing to enlarge their international business quickly, but none has yet taken over a British overseas bank and probably would not be allowed to do so (by the Bank of England).

Altogether, the overseas banks and their subsidiaries maintain more than 3,500 branches in foreign countries. This is the largest network maintained by any country's banking system; it is larger than that of the US banks, although the American banks have long overhauled British banks in terms of the volume of overseas assets and business. This is because the US banks, being comparatively recent arrivals on the international scene, have placed their branches in to-day's business centres only—and not in places where they are likely to be nationalized soon.

Historically, this overseas branch network of the UK banks has had two characteristics: first, the branches were often designed to conduct "retail" banking business in the territories concerned; secondly, each bank in the past tended to specialize in a certain part or parts of the world. Both these characteristics derived from the historical development of the British overseas banks. Set up mainly in the days of the British Empire in the nineteenth century, their function was primarily to serve the needs of traders and then of the settlers in the colonies (like their counterparts in French Africa). They therefore opened branches not only in the main centres, but also throughout the countryside, and began to offer banking services on the same model as the domestic English banks did at home. Naturally they also specialized in certain parts of the world: Barclays International is still strong in Africa and the Caribbean; National and Grindlays in India, the Far East and East Africa; Lloyds and Bolsa in Latin America and Europe.

In the generation after the Second World War, there were many fears for the future of these banks. The difficulties were obvious. The rise of nationalism across the world, and the natural claims of emergent countries for a firmer control of their own economic development, inevitably led not only to closer local control, usually developing into majority interest—and sometimes outright nationalization—but also to the proliferation of exchange regulations, taxation requirements and varying monetary policies. These threatened the business of overseas banks both directly—where their branches were taken over or put under local control—and also indirectly, by loosening the link with London and thus the ability of these banks to switch funds freely from one part of their overseas operations to another. The long succession of crises over the pound sterling was a further burden on them.

However, these years also witnessed the growth of new varieties of international banking: longer-term finance, both for exports and economic development; the servicing of international companies and subsidiaries of European and American companies in Asia, Africa, South America, Australia; the growth of international capital flows; financial advice in all its varied forms. This has all brought further competition for the British overseas banks, which were not well-equipped to provide these kinds of service in the immediate post-war years. At that time, and indeed throughout the 1950s and early 1960s, the dangers confronting them were more apparent than the opportunities. Too many looked like hang-overs from the days of the British Empire.

It needs to be stressed that by 1970, many of these banks had managed to transform themselves into true international banks. The continued growth in their assets and profitability showed their resilience. Instead of merely offering deposit banking services in overseas countries, and trade finance, many of them came to provide a broad range of international banking services of the type described above.

This transformation required several distinct policy steps. First, it was necessary to build up the London base and resources; here Bolsa (the Bank of London and South America, which is now the core of Lloyds and Bolsa International) was amongst the first to see this necessity and act on it—notably by committing itself deeply in the Euro-currency business at a time when many other banks were keeping it at arm's length; now all the British overseas banks have large operations in London's "new" money markets. Second, it was necessary to broaden and modernize the range of services available at the centre, despite difficulties in recruiting staff with the necessary experience; one solution, adopted by National and Grindlays, was to acquire control of a merchant bank (in this case, Wililam Brandts and Sons). Third, it was necessary to build up branches in Europe and America; this process has not been completed yet, but several of these banks have active branches in New York, Germany, and France, and subsidiaries in California. Fourth, several banks acquired new banking partners which gave them access to dollars and business opportunities as mentioned above. Fifth, some banks have amalgamated in order to gain larger resources and spread the risks involved in this kind of overseas business (e.g. Standard and Chartered). Sixth, most of the overseas banks have set up special subsidiaries to offer long-term development finance, aimed at the needs of the developing countries; some have broadened the services available in overseas territories in other ways also; in other words, these banks are attempting to increase the sophistication of the services they offer overseas, so that they will continue to be useful to their "host" countries even if indigenous "local" banks are able to provide the routine banking services. Indeed, due to political pressure, many developing countries are insisting that they should control domestic banks. But even where UK overseas banks have had to surrender control of their branches, they have often retained a presence through these merchant-banking type subsidiaries. Finally, it is worth stressing that only a minority of the total branches or subsidiaries of the banks are in the "vulnerable" developing countries: a very large number are in the economically advanced regions of South Africa, and Australia; many others are in Latin America, the USA, or the Far East. Thus the process of adaption is far advanced, if not yet quite complete.

DEVELOPMENT OF THEIR ACTIVITIES—THE STATISTICS

Table 12, which is compiled from the official statistics published by the Bank of England, shows the development of the business of the members of the British Overseas and Commonwealth Banks Association. The members of this association include many other banks besides the British overseas banks (notably the London offices of Canadian and Australian banks) so it cannot be taken as an exact record of the business development of the British overseas banks themselves. However, they do form the largest single element in the statistics.

With this in mind, it is possible to deduce the general character of their business from these statistics. It may be seen, first of all, that these banks receive large amounts of deposits, in sterling, from overseas residents: £929 millions in March, 1972. This reflects the operation of the sterling system. Non-official overseas holders of sterling keep the main part of their holdings in current and deposit account balances with London banks (whereas central monetary institutions keep their sterling balances mainly in the form of Treasury bills); about half of all non-official balances are in fact held with British overseas and Commonwealth banks—and as the table shows, these balances declined between 1965 and 1969 as the sterling crisis put a strain on the whole system. The table also shows how rapidly these banks have built up their foreign currency deposits in recent years—both directly from overseas residents (to the equivalent of more than £3,000 millions) and from other banks (£1,000 millions).

Turning to the assets side of their balance sheet, it is equally apparent how quickly these banks have increased their activities in the money markets—like all the other "wholesale" banks in London. Balances with other UK banks (in sterling and foreign currencies) bounced up from £349 millions in 1962 to £1,500 millions in 1969, and to £2,000 millions in 1972. Sterling loans to UK local authorities increased from £78 millions to £481 millions. Meanwhile, the volume of their assets placed in "traditional" liquid assets such as money at call and short notice (mainly with the discount market), and sterling bills of exchange declined, at least until the end of 1971 when these banks, like all others, started having to observe the $12\frac{1}{2}$ per cent reserve asset ratio. Advances to UK residents were under official restraint in the later 1960s whilst their deposits increased, so these banks, like the merchant banks, were able to expand their banking business with UK companies quite rapidly when the credit restraints were relaxed in 1971. Yet in the event, demand proved fairly sluggish inside Britain, and the real growth remained in the Euro-currency areas.

BRITISH OVERSEAS BANKS

Barclays Bank International had group deposits at end-September, 1971, of over £2,400 millions and the balance sheet total was about £2,700 millions. It is wholly owned by Barclays Bank Limited, the clearing bank. Before autumn 1971, the bank was known as Barclays Bank DCO and was owned 55 per cent by the clearing bank, which then acquired full ownership. Barclays Bank International has over 1,500 offices in 40 countries Among its main subsidiaries are Barclays National Bank Ltd. which in 1971 became incorporated in South Africa and accounts for between a quarter and a third of the bank's whole business; Barclays Bank of California, with 29 branches; Barclays Bank of New York; and subsidiaries in Uganda, Nigeria, Ghana, Sierra Leone and Zambia. In Malawi, it joined with the Standard Bank to form the National Bank of Malawi, and in 1972 similar plans were afoot in Kenya. In Europe, it has branches in Hamburg and Frankfurt and France and an affiliate in Geneva. The remainder of its banking offices are in many parts of Africa, the Mediterranean (Cyprus, Gibraltar and Malta) and the Caribbean. Like other overseas banks, it expects that governments in developing countries will increasingly wish to acquire a majority stake in its banking operation there. This will tend to reduce the overall size of the bank, but not necessarily its profitability.

The Standard and Chartered Banking Group had deposits of some £2,500 millions at March 31, 1972, and total assets of about £2,800 millions. It resulted from the merger in 1970 of the Standard Bank and the Chartered Bank, but at the time of writing (1972) only some head office activities were being merged. Overseas the banks continued to develop separately. In Europe the group was represented in Hamburg, Paris, Milan, Zurich and Rotterdam.

The Standard Bank operated traditionally mainly in Africa where it has recently been affected by the general process of local incorporation of banks and participation by governments. Its main subsidiary is the Standard Bank of South Africa; there is also the Standard Bank of West Africa, and other subsidiaries in Nigeria, Ghana, Uganda, Zambia and Sierra Leone.

The bank also has large minority interests in the following banks: Banco Standard Totta de Angola, a commercial bank in Angola; Union Zairoise de Banques, a commercial bank operating in the territory formerly known as the Congo, in which the Banque de Bruxelles also has an interest; and Etablissement Financier de Placements, a company based on Switzerland which offers investment management services. The bank also has interests in finance companies and merchant banks in several parts of Africa, and a merchant bank in Kenya (East Africa Acceptances). Apart from the branches operated by the subsidiaries in Africa, the Standard Bank also has, with Chase Manhattan Bank, an affiliate in the Channel Islands; and the Malta International Banking Corporation. The Standard Bank is joined with the Midland Bank, Toronto-Dominion Bank and Commercial Bank of Australia in ownership of Midland and International Banks, the London-based medium-term lending bank.

The Chartered Bank traditionally operated mainly in India, Singapore, Hong Kong and other places in the Far East and South East Asia. Its most important subsidiaries are the Eastern Bank (now changing its name to Chartered) which has about 20 branches, mainly in the Middle East; and the Chartered Bank of

London, which is a bank operating in California. It has a merchant bank in Singapore as well as many branches there; and branches also in Cyprus, Southern Yemen, Ceylon, Malaysia, Brunei, Indonesia, Vietnam, Thailand, Philippines, Hong Kong, China, Korea and Japan. Chartered Bank has an interest in a British merchant bank, Arbuthnot Latham, which traditionally specializes in commodity finance, the Hodge Group of Cardiff, and the Anglo-Nordic Bank in Zurich.

Lloyds and Bolsa International, which is controlled by Lloyds Bank, emerged in 1971 from the union of the Bank of London and South America with Lloyds Bank Europe. It has deposits (September, 1971), of about £1,500 millions. Bank of London and South America was unique among the British overseas banks in that its overseas branches were mainly outside the sterling area and in countries which have never been part of the British Commonwealth. It was one of the most adventurous overseas banks. It was amongst the pioneers of new techniques in international banking, and arranged many large loans to finance developments in Latin America and elsewhere. It was one of the largest operators in the Euro-dollar market and in the secondary market for Euro-bonds. An American bank—Mellon Bank International—held an interest for a number of years before selling it, to Lloyds, in 1973. The present LBI group has inherited this character, and must now be regarded as the international arm of Lloyds Bank. It has interests in many overseas banks and finance companies; these are mainly in South America, though it also has financial subsidiaries in the Netherlands (Arnold Gilissen's Bank) and in Australia, Belgium, France and the Channel Islands. It owns the Bank of London and Montreal, operating in the Caribbean and Central America. Together with its subsidiaries, LBI has branches in New York, Switzerland (3), France (13), Germany (1), Netherlands (3), Belgium (2), Portugal (5), Spain (6) and in most South American countries: namely, Argentina (30), Brazil (14), Colombia (18), Paraguay (8), Peru (2), Uruguay (18), Venezuela (11) and about 30 others in the Caribbean and Central America.

National and Grindlays Bank has also been developing its business in London rapidly in recent years, at the same time as maintaining a large branch network overseas. Lloyds Bank, the clearing bank, owns 41 per cent of the shares of the holding company which, in its turn, holds 60 per cent of the shares of the bank itself. First National City Bank of New York has a 40 per cent interest in the bank itself. Deposits of National and Grindlays Holdings were £850 millions at December 31, 1971 and the balance sheet total was over £1,000 millions. The bank has two merchant bank subsidiaries in Europe, William Brandt's Sons & Co. in London, and Grindlay Brandts SA in Switzerland. National and Grindlays has connections with banks operating in many parts of Africa, the Middle East and far East. In recent years, it has had to relinquish control over its former branches in several countries, as have other British overseas banks. It operates itself many banking offices in India and Pakistan, and others in Rhodesia, Cyprus and several more in the Middle East.

Hong Kong and Shanghai Banking Corporation is one of the largest overseas banks, with total assets at December 31, 1971, of about £2,000 millions (group figures) and is operated from Hong Kong. The principal subsidiaries are the Mercantile Bank which has about 50 branches in East and South-East Asia; the British Bank of the Middle East (managed from London) which has a branch in Switzerland and about 30 other branches throughout the Arab countries of the Middle East; the Hong Kong Bank of California with nine branches in California; the Bank of Iran and the Middle East, a commercial bank with several branches based on Teheran; and the Hang Seng Bank, a commercial bank in Hong Kong. The bank itself has branches in Paris and Hamburg, an office in Australia and over 100 other branches in the East—mainly in Hong Kong (62), but also in Japan, China, Shanghai, India, Indonesia, East and West Malaysia, Singapore, Brunei, Thailand, Vietnam (and the USA). In conjunction with National Westminster Bank, Royal Bank of Canada and Morgan Grenfell (the London merchant bank), it owns the RoyWest Banking Corporation. which provides merchant banking services in the Bahamas. And it has a share in the International Commercial Bank (a bank offering medium-term Euro-dollar loans and other services).

The National Bank of New Zealand is also sometimes included; it is owned by Lloyds Bank and has a large London operation, as well as a network of branches in New Zealand. Total assets at end-1971 were £197 millions.

The Australia and New Zealand Banking Group, which is incorporated in England and administered in Australia, has some 1,500 offices in Australia, New Zealand, the Pacific and the UK.

Part II

D. Foreign Banks in London

Foreign banks have for a long time played an intriguing role in the activities of the City of London. The view in London has always been that, though foreign banks may bring greater competition for English banks, they also bring business to the City and therefore help to build up its international status—a view backed by the historical evidence. So the Bank of England has always kept the door open to the establishment of branches, subsidiaries or offices of foreign-owned banks.

HISTORICAL ROLE

French banks were the first to set up offices in London on the modern pattern: these were the Comptoir National d'Escompte, Crédit Lyonnais and Société Générale in the 1860s. The Banque de Paris opened in London in 1873. These banks quickly became active. Within three years of its establishment in London, for example, Crédit Lyonnais was employing 73 people at its premises in Lombard Street, and shortly afterwards a second branch was opened in the West End of London. By the end of the nineteenth century there was a flourishing foreign banking community in London.

Many more foreign banks were to come in before 1914. Among these were the three big German banks (the Deutsche Bank, the Dresdner Bank and the Disconto Gesellschaft), Italian banks (Banca Commerciale Italiana and the Credito Italiano) and the Russian banks (the Russian Bank for Foreign Trade, Russian Commercial and Industrial Bank and the Russo-Asiatic Bank).

The reasons for this influx are clear. First, London was the undisputed financial centre of the world; the City of London had become the major source of long and short-term finance; the bulk of the world's trade was financed in sterling and the business was profitable. Secondly, some foreign banks undoubtedly took advantage of the fact that the big British deposit banks did not operate branches overseas at that time (though the British Overseas Banks were already established, see above), and did not have departments specializing in foreign business.

The bread-and-butter business of the foreign banks was then the finance of international trade, notably acceptance business. However, they also took part in London's flourishing business in raising loans for overseas borrowers; in some years immediately before the First World War Britain was providing an amount equivalent to some 10 per cent of its total gross national product in overseas capital exports—an incredible sum—most of which was raised on the London capital market. The foreign banks were frequently large subscribers to international bond issues. They also naturally found it convenient to invest, in London, surplus funds arising from their business and that of their customers. It became customary for traders and banks all over the world to keep working balances in London, with its wide range of investment opportunities and its developed money markets.

The First World War closed this chapter in the City's history. Nevertheless, the number of foreign banks continued to increase during the inter-war years (though the German banks did not return), and during the 1920s there was a brief return to the prosperity of the pre-war years. There were particularly profitable opportunities in international arbitrage operations. Several big American banks first opened offices in London. But all the foreign banks suffered during the severe depression of the early 1930s: the volume of international trade contracted, the outflow of capital from Britain dried up and restrictions on trade and investment grew up everywhere.

During the Second World War, the business of the foreign banks in London inevitably dwindled still further and several closed down, including the branches of the Japanese and Italian banks. (Both Japanese and the Italian banks have since returned.) After the war, the banks re-established their connections again in Europe as rapidly as possible, but the host of restrictions on their business and lending opportunities meant that their growth for several years was sluggish. It was not until the return, at the end of the 1950s, to freedom in exchange policies, with the coming of convertibility, and freedom in domestic lending, that the modern structure of foreign banks in London began to develop.

GROWTH IN THE PAST TEN YEARS

In 1957, about 80 foreign banks had direct representation in London; by 1965, this number had reached over 100; by the beginning of 1970, it totalled over 150, and some two years later—by late 1972—it was well over 240. Approximately 200 had branches and representative offices, the remainder had interests in London banks, or in international banks with representation in London. For several years past, *The Banker* has compiled a list of foreign banks in London, and its latest is given in Table 17 together with their date of establishment.

Far more foreign banks are represented in London than in any of the world's other financial centres. In New York, their development was until quite recently hampered by legal restrictions, in Paris by exchange control regulations on the movement of capital, and in Germany, by political considerations and a lack of supporting services.

Another way in which foreign banks have gained a foothold in London is by taking an equity interest in a British bank. Table 18 gives the position at end-1972, and this list *excludes* banks in which British shareholders have minority interests, such as many banks specializing in particular aspects of international finance—notably medium-term Euro-currency operations. (These are given in Table 19.) Foreign banks, notably American banks, have also acquired interests in large old-established British banks; the First National City Bank of New York has an interest in National and Grindlays Bank (see the section on British overseas banks, page 72), and Chase Manhattan Bank has an interest in Standard and Chartered Bank Group.

The best indicator of the importance of the foreign banks in London is the growth of the volume of business. Table 13 shows the increase in their deposits (broken down between deposits of overseas residents and British residents) and in their advances to UK residents between 1955 and March, 1972. It will be seen that total deposits of all the foreign banks combined increased from £263 millions in 1955 to over £12,000 millions in 1969, and, fantastically, to nearly £20,000 millions in 1972, and that most of this immense increase took place in the five most recent years. Their total deposits are now larger than those of the English deposit banks and 40 per cent greater than those of the British merchant banks, overseas banks and other banks. In considering these figures, it is, however, necessary to bear in mind that the great bulk of the foreign banks' deposits are in *foreign currency* and reflect their participation in the Euro-currency markets. Their role in Britain's domestic finances is more accurately reflected in the figures for deposits of and advances to UK residents. It may be seen from the table that in this respect also there has been a considerable expansion: deposits of UK residents have increased from £39 millions in 1955 to £600 millions in 1972, and advances to UK residents from £45 millions to £1,500 millions.

But it was beginning to look as if the British-owned banks were regaining ground in domestic business. Advances to UK residents by foreign banks in Britain still represent, moreover, less than 15 per cent of total advances by all banks to UK residents. These figures exclude short-term loans to local authorities and the money market, and so are a good guide to the volume of commercial lending in sterling to British customers—mainly large and medium-sized companies.

THE BUSINESS OF THE FOREIGN BANKS

The business of the foreign banks in London is of four principal types:

1. They act as international bankers to companies in England and overseas.
2. They are large operators in the short-term money markets, both in sterling and in foreign currencies.
3. They grant loans and credits to finance international trade, development projects overseas and domestic business operations as well as customers in Britain and overseas.
4. They operate as exchange dealers; in this way, they are an integral part of London's foreign exchange market.

Most of the foreign banks came originally in order to gain access to sterling resources and to the wide range of facilities available in London, such as insurance and shipping facilities, with the aim of increasing their ability to meet the needs of their customers. The finance of international trade by traditional techniques of credit such as the acceptance and discounting of bills of exchange continues to be one of their functions.

The major part of the growth in their resources has, however, been in foreign currencies; foreign banks have, indeed, captured the largest share of the Euro-dollar market (see page 106).

Banks employ these Euro-dollar deposits in four main ways. First, they may re-lend them, on the European inter-bank market, to other banks; the profit margins on this type of business are very narrow, not sufficient to cover overhead costs. Secondly, they may make dollar loans direct to commercial customers—mainly international companies—at rates varying according to the term of the loan and the degree of risk. A wide variety of techniques has been evolved to meet the needs of European companies, either for short-term trade finance or for longer-term working capital. In this longer-term area, the Euro-dollar market shades into the Euro-bond market (see Part III), where the foreign banks in London are also active. Recent years have also seen the establishment of a number of co-operative ventures by groups of international banks with the purpose of providing medium-term Euro-dollar funds to European companies (see page 90 and Table 19). Third, in the case of the American banks in London, they may transfer dollars recruited there back to head offices in the United States. The extent to which this is profitable for them depends on the relative cost of short-term funds in the London and New York money markets (after adjustments for any difference in reserve requirements); but United States banks have certainly found it useful to have access to dollars in Europe in case of shortage at home.

In each of these three ways foreign banks balance their foreign currency liabilities in London with foreign currency assets. However, a fourth way in which foreign banks employ Euro-currency deposits is by switching them into sterling for investment in England. The extent to which this is done depends on the level of interest rates in the United Kingdom compared with those in other centres; since most of these funds are covered against possible movements in the "spot" rate, the cost of cover in the forward market also has to be taken into account, as does the general climate of confidence in sterling. During the 1950s, the most important comparison was between the interest yield on British Government Treasury Bills against that on US Treasury Bills. During the 1960s, the most important comparison was that between the interest available on UK local authority deposits against that on Euro-dollar deposits of a comparable term. A description of these markets is given in Part III.

But nowadays, perhaps their biggest role is to act as full international bankers to companies, and individuals—an activity involving a range of services which might be organized and co-ordinated from London rather than from the head office of the bank concerned. These services would include not only finance and advice on international operations, but also economic and market research, setting up contacts for customers, etc. They have made a determined bid for the custom of UK companies. Though their growth has been held back by official credit policy, their resources and advances in sterling recorded a considerable expansion in the five years to mid-1971, as mentioned above. Details are shown in Tables 14, 15 and 16. This growth in their sterling deposits followed from their decision in the early 1960s not to adhere any longer to the deposit banks' agreement then in force, to offer only one rate for time deposits—2 per cent below Bank Rate. By contrast, the foreign banks, like the merchant banks and British overseas banks, offered competitive rates for time deposits.

As a result, the average cost of their funds is higher than it is for the big branch banks like Barclays or National Westminster. Nevertheless, the foreign banks were still able to make advances at competitive rates, for two reasons: first, their overhead costs remained lower than those of the deposit banks (with their big branch networks) in part because they need not process the large number of small accounts that the deposit banks had to handle; secondly, the foreign banks, like other "wholesale" banks, earned higher rates on their liquid assets. Whereas the deposit banks held their non-cash reserves in Treasury bills, commercial bills and loans to the discount market, the foreign banks held their liquid assets mainly in the form of loans to UK local authorities and balances with other banks, where interest yields were appreciably higher.

THE DIFFERENT GROUPS OF FOREIGN BANKS IN LONDON

The official statistics divide the foreign banks into three groups: American banks, "foreign banks and affiliates" (mainly European banks) and "other" foreign banks. The principal balance sheet items of each of these groups are set out in Tables 14, 15 and 16.

The American banks

This is clearly the largest group. There were in 1972 over 40 US banks with branches in the City, and many of them operated two full branches: (see list in Table 17). Within this group, a few banks stood out by virtue of the size of their business, notably

First National City Bank, Chase Manhattan Bank, Bankers Trust Company, Bank of America, Morgan Guaranty Trust Company and Manufacturers Hanover Trust Company. All these opened offices in London before the Second World War. Apart from the Bank of America, which is the world's largest bank and has its head office in California, they all come from New York. In the late 1950s and 1960s they were joined by other banks from New York and other centres on the East Coast; but since then many banks from other parts of the United States, notably from the West Coast, and other industrial centres, have entered London. A main reason for this was that many "inland" banks feared that they might lose valuable business to the New York banks unless they too could provide a full international service. They also needed to have access to the Euro-dollar market. For both reasons, they had to be in London. For several of these banks, London is their only foreign branch; and although the bigger banks have a branch network that covers the entire world, London is for all of them the most important foreign centre.

The influx of the American banks was watched with close attention in the City (apart from any other consideration, their need to recruit experienced staff resulted in a rapid increase in the salaries offered to foreign exchange dealers and other experts). It is all the more important to place their role in perspective. As Table 14 shows, the extraordinary increase in their total deposits from £96 millions in 1951 and £454 millions in 1962 to about £10,000 millions in 1969 and nearly £14,000 millions in 1972, was due overwhelmingly to foreign currency business, where they were not directly competing with the deposit banks. True the table shows that their advances to UK residents totalled about £1,000 millions in March, 1972. This was nearly 10 per cent of total advances by all banks to UK residents. Moreover, if it is assumed that their lending was exclusively to UK companies, then their share in total bank advances to UK-resident companies was about 15 per cent. These banks now lend more to UK residents in sterling than do the British overseas banks (see Table 12) or the merchant banks (see Table 11). So their role in domestic bank credit is significant, and will almost certainly continue to grow, but it is not yet a preponderant one even in the corporate sector. Looked at from another angle, the role of the US banks corresponds broadly to that of US-controlled companies in the British economy.

In banking techniques, the American banks certainly brought several new ideas to the City. It was their introduction of dollar certificates of deposit that led to the development of sterling certificates of deposit. Drawing on their experience with the financial problems of large multi-national corporations, they developed techniques for minimizing the amount of cash "float" which such corporations need to maintain; in this respect the Big Three US banks—First National City, Chase Manhattan and Bank of America—had a particular advantage in that they could transfer funds instantaneously to any part of the world through their branch networks. The US banks also employed "business school" techniques of cash flow credit analysis on which to base their lending judgments; with this, they promoted the "term loan"—where the loan is for a fixed amount, to be normally repaid by regular agreed instalments at a fixed interest rate. Their use of economists and other specialist advisors has been an example to many English banks. Finally, the volume and skill of their advertising and bank salesmanship came as a revelation (perhaps a disquieting one) to many English bankers.

Some American banks are certainly considering whether to widen the services they offer in the United Kingdom further. Already they have entered the fields of merchant banking, computer leasing, factoring, travel services, credit cards and investment management. Several of them have set up branches in provincial centres such as Birmingham, Manchester and Belfast. Some were in 1972 campaigning for deposits even more agressively than previously from individuals. Yet on balance, it was beginning to look as if the penetration of US banks into domestic banking had reached its high water-mark. In 1972 they were not making quite so much noise as previously.

The European banks

The principal European banks represented in London are members of an association—more or less a club—called "Foreign Banks and Affiliates Association". Members include banks from France, Spain, the Netherlands, Belgium, Greece, Switzerland, Czechoslovakia—and the Bank of China. Most of these banks have been established in London for many years, either with branches or affiliates. Table 15 shows the development of this group of banks according to the official statistics.

These banks in the past engaged mainly in financing trade and providing banking services to people from their home country who were carrying on business in England, or with English firms, or simply visiting. Spanish banks, for instance, are still heavily engaged in financing the import into England of fruit and other produce from Spain and Spanish-speaking countries.

These banks were also, naturally, active in the Euro-dollar market—above all the Swiss banks but also the French, Belgian and Dutch banks and others. Table 15 shows that their deposits in foreign currencies from overseas residents increased at an extraordinary rate between 1965 and 1969; by contrast, their advances to overseas residents did not then increase so rapidly. In their money-market operations, these banks were at that time acting as a channel for the recruitment of Euro-dollar funds in Europe which they then lent to London branches of American banks (this shows up, in the table, in the rapid growth of the item "balances with other UK banks"). Their sterling business (deposits and advances to UK residents in sterling) has also been growing quite quickly, but is still relatively small. On the other hand, they have been extending their activities in the sterling money market.

In general, the statistics relating to this group of banks do not show the fantastic growth of the American banks in London; nevertheless, their operations are on a large scale and the growth has been impressive. Many of these banks have large establishments in London; British and French Bank, an affiliate of Banque Nationale de Paris, employed 250 people in 1971, and Banque Belge (the affiliate in London of Société Générale de Banque), the Crédit Lyonnais and Société Générale have establishments of about 200 people; the Algemene Bank Nederland and the Bank of China each have staffs totalling about 100 people.

Other overseas banks

This is a heterogeneous group comprising all the other foreign banks which maintain banking offices in London: notably the Japanese banks and the banks listed in Table 17 from Afghanistan, Thailand, India, Cyprus. Iran, Pakistan, Malaysia, Singapore, Iraq and other countries.

One of the largest and most interesting banks in this group is the Moscow Narodny Bank. This is actually an English bank and is operated, with great success, on impeccable capitalist principles; but it is owned and controlled by Soviet organizations. Its operations in London, where it has built up a first-class reputation, are on a very extensive scale. Its basic purpose is the finance and promotion of trade between East and West. With the increasing size of industrial plants, it has also extended an increasing volume of medium-term funds to Eastern European countries and has experienced no difficulty in raising the finance required. It plays a large part in the Euro-dollar market—indeed, it was one of the pioneers of the Euro-dollar market back in the 1950s. It issues certificates of deposit both in dollars and sterling.

The other very active banks in this group are the Japanese banks—about a dozen of which have branches in the City. Since Japanese trade is still financed to a large extent in dollars—and Japanese companies have been prominent at certain times both as borrowers and sometimes as massive lenders in the international markets—it is naturally important for these banks to have access to the Euro-dollar market.

The growth in the business of this group of banks between 1965 and 1972 and the breakdown of their assets and liabilities is shown in Table 16. It will be seen that they do not conduct much business with UK residents (either on the side of deposits or on that of advances), and that their operations in sterling generally are limited. The overwhelming part of their resources comes from foreign currency deposits, either from overseas residents or from other banks in London and the bulk of their assets is devoted to foreign currency advances to overseas residents, or in "balances with other UK banks" (which are largely in foreign currencies). They do not hold any large portfolio of sterling bills of exchange, or of British Government securities; nor do they lend on a large scale to UK local authorities, or other sterling money markets. In other words, these banks do not compete with British banks for UK business.

Comparing Tables 14, 15 and 16, it is clear that the American banks are the largest foreign banks in London, and that they are growing most rapidly. Their total deposits (sterling and currency) in London in 1972 stood at about £14,000 millions, compared with £3,200 millions for the "foreign banks and affiliates"—that is, the European banks—and £2,500 millions for the others. It is the American banks, also, that pose the most serious threat to British banks—the merchant banks and deposit banks; in the figures, this is seen in the big increase in sterling deposits with them. The glamour of the US banks should not blind us, however, to the importance of the other 150 foreign banks in London; certainly from the point of view of these banks themselves, the London branch often acts as the pivot of their international operations, helping them to service trade and investment not only between their own home country and the United Kingdom, but also in many other parts of the world.

From the point of view of British banks, the presence of these foreign banks helps to keep London in touch with the constantly changing conditions in other countries and the changing needs and customs of traders. Taken together, they constitute a vast reservoir of accumulated knowledge, experience and contacts: a reservoir constantly being refreshed by the ceaseless interchange of personal visits, lunches, conversations and friendship at every level. Through such contacts, it is possible in London to find out, instantaneously, the latest economic and political developments in almost any country in the world—and bankers' views of them. It is this personal communication that is the real secret behind the huge banking business discussed in this chapter.

EUROCURRENCY CONSORTIA BANKS

These consortia banks, which are owned jointly by other banks usually from a variety of countries, were established in considerable numbers in London in 1967-72. They differ considerably from each other in many respects. Their original purpose was, essentially, to act as a channel for the provision of large-scale funds at medium term (which has come to mean anything between 2 years and 10) to international companies, governments and government agencies round the world. In providing such credits, the banks may utilize their own resources, or ask their shareholding banks to participate, or invite outside banks to do so, or attract funds in the money markets (a portion of such lending is financed by short-term deposits). Interest rates charged on such loans normally fluctuate during the term of the loan, being altered every 3 to 6 months to a previously-agreed fixed margin above the prevailing level of short-term rates in London. See page 110 and Table 19.

Part II

E. Other Banks and Near-Banks

Apart from the groups of great banks already described, there are a number of other banks and "near-banks" in the United Kingdom. The National Giro system, for instance, was opened in 1968 and is operated on similar lines to the Giro system in many European countries. It was designed to provide a cheap and rapid money transfer service for individuals who did not have a bank account, and also has attractions for companies. It has slowly built up its resources and the number of its customers; the big clearing banks certainly have reason to watch carefully the growth of this new service, which does provide competition for them. But it has made large losses. Its very existence was for a time in doubt after the Tory election victory in June, 1970, and it has not yet made a major impact on the distribution of deposits and on the financial mechanism; in December, 1971, its deposits totalled only about £70 millions. Moreover, its scale of charges was sharply raised in 1972 (though some types of transaction remained free), prompting some observers to ask whether it still fulfilled its original purpose.

Other important financial intermediaries, or "near-banks", are the building societies, the hire purchase finance companies and the savings banks (The Trustee Savings Bank and the National Savings Bank). The Radcliffe Committee, in its report on the monetary system* put considerable stress on the growth of these financial intermediaries. True, their deposits do not have quite the same quality of "moneyness" as those of the deposit banks. They do, however, represent a large and growing volume of "near money", i.e. of highly liquid claims that easily can be converted into cash.

* Committee on the working of the Monetary System, Report, Cmnd. 827, HMSO, London, 1959.

BUILDING SOCIETIES

Building societies are the chief sources of finance for private house purchase in Britain. At the end of 1971, their total assets were above £13,000 millions, of which the great proportion represented mortgages. There were 467 building societies in the country (end 1971), of which five had assets of over £500 millions; nearly 12 million people had shares or deposits with them, and the number of borrowers was about 3½ million. The average mortgage (i.e. amount borrowed) in 1972 was about £5,000.

The building societies have been growing very rapidly. Their total assets doubled in the five years 1967 to 1972. They finance their lending mainly by attracting deposits from the general public through their branches (of which they have, together, over 2,000). This means that they have to offer competitive rates of interest, in order to be able to meet the demand for mortgages. In early 1972, they offered a rate of 4½ per cent on deposits, but tax on this was paid by the society, so that for depositors it represented a good investment (equivalent to about 7¾ per cent for people paying tax at the standard rate). On new mortgages, most of the societies charged interest at the rate of 8 per cent (after January, 1972); but borrowers obtain relief of income tax on the interest they pay to the building society, so that the true cost to them is usually lower than that. Interest rates, both for borrowers and lenders, are changed from time to time in accordance with the general level of rates in the economy. Even though they were rising again in 1972, there is no doubt that since the last war house purchase has been one of the best investments in England; and it is still the dream of every married couple to have a little house of their own.

HIRE PURCHASE FINANCE COMPANIES

The work of these institutions has already been touched on elsewhere (see Part IIA and Part III). Many of the large finance houses are connected to one of the deposit banks.

Their main business is to lend money to private individuals, directly and indirectly, to help them buy cars and consumer goods. Under a hire purchase agreement, the customer in theory only rents (or hires) the goods; it becomes his property only when the last instalment has been paid; the security, from the point of view of the finance company, is therefore the goods themselves and it has the right to recover the goods if the customer should default on payments of his instalments (though the company must obtain a court order before repossessing the goods, after a certain proportion of the purchase price has been paid). Alternatively, the finance companies may make a personal loan to the customer—an arrangement that has certain advantages over the traditional hire purchase agreement.

In recent years, many of the larger finance companies have diversified into other types of business, such as leasing equipment to companies. Several also have links with finance companies and banks in other countries, in Europe and America. Some have special export finance divisions.

Total outstanding lending of the finance houses was about £1,100 millions at the end of 1971 (on hire purchase and other credit instalment lending). In addition, they advanced another £150 millions or so by way of loans and advances and had £200 millions in leased assets outstanding. They financed this partly by borrowing (mainly from the banks), and partly by attracting deposits; their deposits totalled about £820 millions. Their business grew very rapidly during the 1950s, but was restrained by official monetary policy during much of the 1960s; like the banks, they were subject to official "ceilings" on the amounts they may lend. They have also been affected by official controls on the *terms* of hire purchase agreements (specifying the maximum repayment period and the minimum deposit allowed).

In 1971 these controls were relaxed, and late in that year, the growing similarity of the business of banks and some finance houses was officially recognized when the latter were made subject to reserve asset requirements, like the banks, though at a lower rate of 10 per cent (of eligible liabilities) rather than 12½ per cent applied to the banks. This means they were brought into the framework of official banking regulations. Some large houses at that time decided to apply for full banking status, partly for prestige reasons and partly because it would enable them to do some new kinds of business.

THE NATIONAL SAVINGS MOVEMENT

The National Savings movement consists principally of two kinds of savings bank—the Trustee Savings Banks and the National Savings Bank—and special securities and savings services offered by the Government for the "small saver": such as, National Savings Certificates and Premium Bonds. The following description is based on an official account*.

* *The British Banking System*, HMSO, London——————
The statistics and some other details have been brought up to date.

TRUSTEE SAVINGS BANKS

Trustee savings banks are local banks and can be found in most of the cities and larger towns in Britain. In July, 1972, there were 73 trustee savings banks in Britain with 1,524 offices—over 10½ million people now have savings bank accounts; the total funds held by the trustee savings banks amounted to about £3,079 millions. The trustee savings banks are linked together through the Trustee Savings Bank Association, which is endowed with various co-ordinating powers. The banks are inspected by the Trustee Savings Bank Inspection Committee, a statutory body which submits an annual report to Parliament.

Trustee savings banks maintain two departments: the "ordinary" and "special investment" departments. Deposits in the ordinary department yielded interest currently (in 1972) of 3½ per cent: deposits in the special investment department, of up to £10,000 on which a higher rate of interest is paid, (generally around 7 per cent in 1972) are allowed provided the depositor has at least £50 in the ordinary department.

Income tax relief is given on the first £21 of interest (£42 in the case of a married couple's joint account) on deposits in the ordinary department. A depositor may not deposit money in more than one trustee savings bank. Withdrawal arrangements vary to some extent from bank to bank; deposits are normally repayable up to £50 on demand in the case of the ordinary departments, while deposits in the special investment departments are normally subject to one month's notice. Arrangements exist by which depositors can withdraw money through trustee savings banks other than the bank at which their account is held.

Current account service and the use of cheques were first authorized in 1964, and are now offered by the banks. Current accounts are non-interest bearing and depositors are able to draw cheques on them at a fixed charge of 2½p per cheque, subject to an allowance for minimum retained balances of not less than £50. No overdrafts are permitted. Other facilities which the trustee savings banks offer include the sale and purchase of government securities and national savings securities on behalf of their customers; dividends may be automatically credited to their accounts. Many banks will undertake the payment of rates and gas and electricity accounts and the safe custody of securities and valuables.

The funds of the ordinary departments are deposited with the National Debt Commissioners, who invest them in the same way as those of the National Savings Bank (see below). The trustees of the savings banks manage the portfolio of the special investment departments, but each transaction is subject to the approval of the National Debt Commissioners. Just under a half of the deposits of the special investment departments are at present invested in government guaranteed and local authority stocks, while the remainder is invested in loans to local authorities.

The *trustee savings bank unit trust* was set up and operated by the Trustee Savings Bank Association in 1968 and does not carry a government guarantee. All the operating and capital expenses are met from the trust's funds and the savings banks act solely as selling agents, working on commission. The unit trust is in the same position in law as other unit trusts, i.e. is subject to the normal Department of Trade and Industry conditions and requirements.

THE NATIONAL SAVINGS BANK

The National Savings Bank (formerly the Post Office Savings Bank) is one of the largest organizations of its kind in the world, controlling over 22 million active accounts. Post offices throughout the country deal with about 130 million transactions each year, and total deposits at the end of May, 1972 amounted to £1,483 millions, excluding investment accounts (see below).

An account may be opened with a minimum of 25p; deposits are limited to £10,000. Deposits and withdrawals are recorded in the depositor's bank book and they may be made at any of the 21,000 post offices in Britain where savings bank business is transacted. All management and records are centralized at the Head Office. Withdrawals up to £20 may be made on demand at any savings bank post office, and larger amounts may be withdrawn at a few days' notice either in cash at a particular post office, or by crossed warrant payable through a bank. An emergency withdrawal service by telegraph is also available.

Investment accounts were introduced in 1966 with an initial interest rate to depositors of $5\frac{1}{2}$ per cent per annum ($7\frac{1}{2}$ per cent in mid-1972), but investors must have a qualifying £50 deposit in the Ordinary Department and withdrawals are subject to one month's notice. By May, 1972 the amount invested in these accounts was £431 millions. Investment policy has been directed towards the building up of a portfolio of securities calculated to provide the best income consistent with the needs of the fund.

Deposits go into a fund which is handed over to the National

Debt Commissioners for investment in government stock or other special securities covering the outstanding liabilities to depositors. The interest earned by these investments is set against the interest due to depositors and management expenses. The Government guarantees the repayment of the sums invested with accrued interest, when required.

In March 1971 a Committee to Review National Savings was appointed to consider the future role of these banks and their relationship with the government. Its report was eagerly awaited as this book went to press, especially any recommendations it might make to allow these institutions to lend money, determine interest rates, and so become proper banks.

Part III
The Money Markets

London's special role in world finance has frequently been ascribed to its highly developed money markets. The relationship between the banks and the money markets has already been touched upon. This chapter gives a brief description of the main markets in which the banks participate. It is divided into two parts:

A. *The sterling money markets,* which provide means for short-term investment of sterling liquid funds, notably the liquid funds of banks, so that there is never any need for funds to be left "idle", in cash, in the system,

B. *The Euro-currency markets,* ranging from the short-term market in foreign currency deposits to the longer-term Euro-bond market.

There are other financial markets in London like the gold market (see page 66), the foreign exchange market, the ship and air charter market; and the insurance market, which conducts a very large amount of international business. There are also commodity markets in cocoa, coffee, cotton, furs, grains, hides and skins, jute, metals, rubber, shellac, sisal, sugar, tea, vegetable oils and other commodities. But these are outside the scope of the present work, as is the stock exchange and the long-term capital market.

A. THE STERLING MONEY MARKETS

London's money markets have undergone profound changes in recent years. Until the mid-1950s, there was only one important short-term money market—the discount market, provided by the companies forming the Discount Market Association. Then in the 1960s, alongside this "traditional" market there developed several other sterling markets: notably the markets in short-term deposits with local authorities and hire purchase finance houses, and the inter-bank market. Then in the latter part of the 1960s, many brokers and discount houses began operating in both the "old" and the "new" markets. Most recently the change-over to the new credit system in late 1971 (see page 122) encouraged these various markets to mesh again closely into each other so that once again London had a largely untrammelled and diversified money market mechanism. We examine these markets in turn.

The discount market

The discount market is made up of 12 discount houses. Each of these is a public company and is independent of other financial institutions. The houses exist by borrowing money (almost entirely on a day-to-day basis), and investing this money in short-term paper expected to yield a slightly higher rate of interest than the cost of their funds; traditionally, they invested mainly in Treasury bills, commercial bills and government securities (bonds). Recently they have invested also in certificates of deposit (issued by banks), local authority securities, and other assets. For many years they borrowed most of their money from the big deposit (clearing) banks; from the point of view of the banks, this "money at call" lent to the discount market represented, as it still does, their most liquid asset (after cash); it is their first line of reserves, since they know that they can "call" (withdraw) this money at any time if they find themselves short of cash. Since autumn 1971, the houses have also borrowed larger sums from other banks—overseas, foreign and merchant banks—because these banks then had to start maintaining reserve assets, and money at call with the market qualified as such. Banks know that the discount houses, in their turn, can borrow at the last resort from the Bank of England, if at the end of any day there is a shortage of cash in the system as a whole. The discount houses are the only institutions to which the Bank of England lends money "at last resort"; but to them the Bank will lend in any amount necessary to satisfy the public's demand for cash (as channelled through the banking system).

On any given day, it is likely that some banks will need to "call" some funds; others will have a surplus to lend. These different requirements are balanced out through the discount market. If the *overall* supply of money is insufficient on any day for a discount house to balance its books, the Bank of England can relieve the shortage by buying bills (either direct from a discount house or from a bank), or, alternatively, it can make "last resort" loans to the discount market against "eligible" security. The choice between these methods, and the rate of interest charged by the Bank for its loans, will depend mainly on the Bank's view of the appropriate level of interest rates. If the Bank feels that short-term interest rates should rise, it can deliberately engineer a shortage of cash in the system by open-market operations, thus forcing the market to borrow from it, and then charge a high rate (penal rate) for its "last resort" loans. This in turn tends to raise the average cost of money borrowed by the discount houses; they, in their turn, react by lowering the price they bid for Treasury bills at the weekly auction (that is to say, they attempt to buy Treasury bills at a higher effective *yield*) in order to restore the profitability of their operations.

The discount market therefore can be seen as performing several functions:

1. It provides a system through which the ebb and flow of cash in the banking system can be evened out. In England, traditionally, the big deposit banks did not borrow from one another but instead lent to the discount market.

2. It is a channel through which the Bank of England provides additional new cash to the system if there is a demand for it. This may be especially important in times of crisis.

3. It forms part of the mechanism through which the Bank can raise short-term interest rates, if it wishes to.

4. The discount houses provide a specialised market for the buying and selling of accepted bills of exchange, and other money market instruments.

5. The discount houses are important as holders of Government securities (bonds) that are approaching maturity. This business grew up in the inter-war years when the discount houses' business in commercial bills declined, due mainly to the trade depression. Owing to the possibility of large fluctuations in the prices of Government securities, however, bond business has been the source not only of exceptional profits, but also of exceptional difficulties for the discount houses.

The sources of the discount market's borrowed funds and the changes in them between 1958 and 1972 are shown in Table 20. It will be seen that until 1971, the market borrowed most of its funds from the London clearing banks and Scottish banks. In 1958, these sources accounted for 68 per cent of the total; in

1969 they accounted for 80 per cent. But in 1971, the new system of credit control meant that *all* banks had to keep reserve assets, and suddenly the discount market was taking huge sums from accepting houses, overseas banks and other banks. In 1958, 26 per cent of its funds were borrowed from these banks; then, as the table shows, the amount borrowed declined to only 13 per cent in 1968, but by June, 1972, this had soared to 42 per cent. What had happened before 1971, as we shall see in the next section, was that these banks developed other money markets for adjusting their liquidity position, notably the inter-bank market and local authority money market, where their funds earned higher rates than the discount market could offer. The tables of the assets and liabilities of these banks (Tables 11, 12, 14, 15 and 16) show that these banks did not increase their lending to the discount market significantly until 1971 (as shown by the item "Money at call and short notice").

Finally, the discount houses borrow some funds from industrial and commercial companies—mining companies, insurance companies, some industrial concerns and so forth. This, too, has grown recently. A small proportion of the funds borrowed by the discount houses comes direct from overseas.

By tradition, a discount house lodges security against the vast bulk of the money it borrows. And the security which it gives are the bills or bonds in which it has invested its borrowings.

What they invest in

The distribution of the discount market's assets between 1958 and 1972 is shown in Table 21. It will be seen that the market's total assets increased steadily until 1967, and then declined for a year or so, due partly to growth of "new" money markets and partly to the swing from deficit into surplus in the Government's finances (which caused the supply of Treasury bills to dry up).

The outstanding feature of those years was the revival of the commercial bill; this included bank bills, where the bill is accepted by a first-class London bank or accepting house, and "trade bills" (commonly simply drawn by one trader on another). The discount houses eagerly encouraged such business. The supply of bills increased during the "credit squeezes" in the 1960s as traders found it increasingly difficult to obtain credit from other sources (so that, after 1965, official restrictions were also applied to this source of finance). The rates at which discount houses purchase commercial bills vary greatly according to the quality of the bill concerned, but the yield on them is always higher than the current Treasury bill rate. As the table shows, the revival of the commercial bill enabled the market then to compensate for the decline in holdings of Treasury bills and Government bonds: in 1969, commercial bills represented 40 per cent of their total assets.

The discount houses have increased their purchases of bills and bonds issued by UK local authorities. Local authority bills are "eligible" as security for loans from the Bank of England. But then in 1971, with the sudden flood of new money, rates were driven down fast. The funds were invested notably in certificates of deposit—and again in Government securities (the house having to maintain a 50 per cent public debt ratio). The historic rise in their assets in 1971 brought their total portfolio above £3,000 millions.

The discount market has faced many challenges to its prosperity—and even its existence—during its long history. The secret of its survival has been its readiness to adapt to new conditions, as in 1971 and 1972. It is not indispensable. Other ways could be found of evening out the flow of funds between the commercial banks. But the Bank's new money scheme of 1971 ensured it a continuing, and indeed again a central, place in the financial mechanism.

The discount houses have themselves diversified. First, several acquired interests in firms of money brokers specializing either in the new sterling money markets or in foreign currency deposits. Second, discount houses began to deal in types of paper outside their "traditional" assets, as in local authority bonds. They also came to provide a secondary market in certificates of deposit in sterling, and some houses began to operate a market in foreign currency bills of exchange and dollar certificates of deposit. So long as they do not start behaving like ordinary banks, their place is now assured.

The inter-bank market and certificates of deposit

An important development during the 1960s was the evolution of an active inter-bank market in short-term sterling funds. The big deposit banks (clearing banks) did not then participate in it —partly perhaps from a desire to preserve the discount market which was convenient for them in other ways. But most of the other banks in London were active in it from the start—well over 100 in all. These included foreign banks with London offices, merchant banks and some specialized subsidiaries of the clearing banks. The banks used this market to balance out their day-to-day cash and short money positions; so the market fulfilled some of the functions, for these banks, that the discount market did then for the clearing banks. But the market was also used as a general source of funds to support lending to customers.

The mechanism of the market is straightforward. Occasionally banks deal direct with each other, but usually deals are arranged by specialist firms of money brokers such as Guy Butler, Murray-Jones, Charles Fulton and R. P. Martin. As already noted, the discount houses soon entered this market indirectly by taking interests in firms of money brokers.

The size of the individual deals on the inter-bank market go up to several million pounds. The preferred minimum contract is £250,000. The terms of the deals were at first very short: a large proportion overnight and weekend money; much of the rest, three days. Most transactions are still at the short end, but deposits of a wide range of maturities up to 5 years are taken—and deposits of more than 2 years are "reserve free", i.e. there is no requirement to keep reserve assets against them. When dealing through brokers, banks usually let it be known which other banks they do not want to lend to—banks try to keep within the lending limits they have for each bank.

Loans are unsecured—in contrast to the procedure on the discount market. In general, interest rates are higher than on the discount market, though lower than on the local authorities' loans market, and appreciably lower than on the hire purchase finance companies' market. Reflecting the intense competition, profit margins on dealing in this market are small.

This market grew rapidly. Official statistics are not available, but the total outstanding debt in the market may be estimated at around £1,000 millions in 1969, and £4,000 millions in 1972. Certainly the total fluctuates greatly.

The market is the principal link between the various sterling money markets and the Euro-dollar market. It is a key market, and rates in it are watched closely.

Certificates of deposit in sterling were first issued in 1968 and by October 1970 the amount outstanding was just over £1,000 millions. Towards the end of 1971 the clearing banks themselves began issuing CDs and the total outstanding soared upwards to £2,300 millions at end-1971 and to nearly £5,000 millions at end-1972. The great bulk were for periods of between one month and one year, and increasingly the CD market was seen as an enlargement of the inter-bank market—rates were virtually identical. Most CDs were indeed purchased by other banks, though the original idea was to use them to attract funds from outside the banking system; and, as with the inter-bank market as a whole, there were those who questioned the wisdom of banks which relied on such markets too heavily as sources of funds.

The local authority market

The market for short-term loans to local authorities in the UK is, in terms of the funds outstanding, the largest of the "new" money markets in London which grew up in the 1960s alongside the traditional money market run by the discount houses. It was not the result of any conscious attempt to establish a new money market; rather it evolved from the circumstances of the late 1950s.

The first of these was the effective closure of the Public Works Loan Board in 1955. Until the mid-1950s the bulk of the borrowing requirements of Local Authorities in Britain came, in effect, from the central government in the shape of the PWLB. When access to this was severely limited, the councils were forced to borrow on the open market. The second factor was the return to convertibility of sterling and other European currencies in 1958. This freed non-resident sterling balances, which could move in and out of the country at will, and also paved the way for the evolution of Euro-currency markets. A third more general factor was the increasing financial sophistication of large companies, pension funds and other large financial institutions. As a result of these forces, the short-term debt of the local authorities bounded ahead from £130 millions in 1955, to £1,200 millions in 1962, and £1,800 millions in 1965.

In the following four years, the total increased more slowly. In 1964 government concern over the proportion of very short-term debt had led to a partial re-opening of the PWLB and encouragement of other forms of borrowing. The proportion of short-term debt itself was limited by Government order. Nevertheless, borrowings in 1972 were around £2,000 millions.

The borrowers in the market are hundreds of local authorities all over Britain, varying greatly in size and financial sophistication. At one end of the scale there is the Corporation of the City of Westminster, comprising half the centre of London; at the other, a small Scottish borough with a population of, say 3,000.

The main lenders are the conglomeration of banks in the City of London— clearing and merchant banks, British overseas and foreign banks (with £400 millions). Commercial and industrial companies lend £300 millions, while financial institutions like investment trusts, pension funds and building societies provide some £600 millions. The rest comes from private individuals (£300 millions) and other sources. The volume of overseas funds attracted to the market depends on the interest rates offered compared to those ruling in the Euro-currency markets, and the cost of forward cover. Most of the overseas funds are in any case indirect, i.e. placed by banks in London.

Putting these various lenders in touch with the multitude of borrowers is a complex task. It is conducted principally through brokers, although some loans are made direct. The structure of these brokers is varied. Some will deal direct both with borrowers and lenders. But often a second tier of brokers is used. Hence a bank might approach one of the inter-bank brokers who might place the money through one of the specialist local authority brokers. Several of the discount houses have taken interests in money brokers. Brokers earn their income in commission.

The size of the loans varies from less than £100,000 (this is the usual minimum) to £1 million, while blocks of £50 millions have also been placed. The bulk of this money is at very short notice—about £1,500 millions is on seven days or less.

Hire purchase finance company market

Most leading finance companies—basically instalment credit companies—finance their activities partly by bidding for deposits, in large amounts, on the open market. Their need for funds from this source depends on the demand for consumer credit (to finance purchases of motor cars, etc.) within the limits, if any, set by the monetary authorities, and on the other sources of finance available to them. In the last half of the 1960s, the ability of finance houses to expand their lending was then severely restricted by official policy, and for many years their total resources fluctuated around £900 millions to £1,000 millions. But in 1971, their assets rose rapidly as their HP debt outstanding recovered after the easing and then abolition of official restrictions; the volume of goods and equipment leased out to customers—a fast growing element of their business—also bounded ahead. On the liabilities side, deposits rose rapidly during the early 1960s to over £700 millions in 1966, fell slightly in the following three years to around £630 millions in 1969, and then spurted ahead to £823 millions at end-1971. A small portion of this is placed with the finance houses direct by overseas residents; about £350 millions is placed by banks and other financial institutions; about £300 millions by industrial and commercial companies in the United Kingdom; and about £100 millions comes from other UK residents (i.e. the general public). Some of the funds placed by banks probably represent funds from overseas.

The market in deposits with HP companies is, therefore, the smallest of the sterling money markets.

Interest rates offered by companies are, however, the highest available in these markets. Deposits are usually arranged for three or six months. The rate of interest is fixed at the outset for the period of the deposit. The rates offered vary according to the term and size of the deposit and also, since the deposits are unsecured, according to the size and standing of the company concerned; companies with connections to a clearing bank are generally able to command the finest rates. Most large companies obtain these deposits through money brokers without advertising.

The inter-company market in short-term funds

British bankers have long been keeping a watchful eye on the rapid growth in the United States of the so-called "third banking system" made up of non-bank lenders and comprising the major corporations which lend and borrow money from each other, thus bypassing the banks. English bankers prefer to think that the emergence of such a market in the United States is the result of special factors there that do not apply in England—notably the system of "compensating balances" which contributes to the high cost of borrowing from banks there (relative to the general level of money rates). Bank finance is indeed cheap in England, compared to the general level of interest rates. Nevertheless, some large companies in England did begin in the late 1960s to borrow and lend short-term funds to one another. Sometimes the services of an expert money broker are used; sometimes the deal is arranged directly between company treasurers. The original cause of the development of this market was probably the official restrictions on bank lending and the very tight liquidity position of some companies in 1968-69. But the market survived the ending of the credit squeeze in 1971, though after the collapse of one company which had borrowed on the market, there were growing calls for closer supervision by the authorities—and a more open and systematic method of assessing risks in the market itself. Interest rates on such transactions tend to be rather high.

Interest rates in the sterling money markets

The level of interest rates in the money markets is determined by supply and demand. This again is a big change introduced by 1971 reforms. Before then, rates in the old discount market were set mainly by Bank rate; the minimum rate at which the clearing banks lent to the discount market varied, by convention, in accordance with Bank rate.

B. THE EURO-DOLLAR MARKET

This is not the place to attempt a full description of that much discussed phenomenon—the Euro-currencies market. Its importance in this context lies in its considerable impact on British banking.

As is well-known, the growth in this international market has been dramatic. In 1959, when the market was first measured in a systematic way, its size was estimated as probably in excess of $1,000 millions. In 1967, it had reached $17,500 millions (without counting inter-bank deposits). At end-1969, the net size of the market was estimated at $44,000 millions, but by 1972 it had grown to $82,000 millions. The Euro-dollar market comprises some four-fifths of the market in Euro-currencies.

It is often said that it owed its origin to the preference of East European countries for holding their dollars in banks in Europe rather than in the United States towards the end of the 1950s. Also, in 1957 British banks were given a special incentive to accept dollar deposits in order to make dollar loans to finance overseas trade among non-sterling area countries, since the use of sterling for such purposes was forbidden in 1957. Another specific reason was the effect of Regulation Q, which limited the rate of interest that American banks could pay for deposits in the United States (whilst American *lending* rates remained quite high). As the Bank of England described it in the mid-1960s:

> "Banks in London have been able to attract large sums in dollars by quoting better rates for deposits, including money at call and short notice—categories which earn nothing at all with New York banks—and have employed them at less than the US lending rate and still made a worthwhile turn. They

are able to operate on a fairly small profit margin because the additional overhead expenses of conducting their Euro-dollar activities are minimal."*

More general influences were the move towards external convertibility in Europe in 1958 and the continuing US payments deficit, which put a continuing flow of dollars into the hands of non-residents.

But it can be argued that additional reasons are necessary to explain the truly extraordinary growth of the market. This new form of international banking may well owe much of its attractiveness to the rigidities and restraints on existing banking activities, not only in the United States but also in Europe. These restraints included the agreement between banks in several European countries on interest rates (both on deposits and advances) and restrictions imposed by European monetary authorities on domestic banking. Banks operating with dollars have been able to exploit these rigidities; the dollar market has certainly had a large impact on interest rates in other centres, and especially in those countries where holders of domestic currencies are permitted to switch into Euro-dollars.

London is the centre of the Euro-dollar market. At the end of 1971, deposits at London banks denominated in foreign currencies totalled about £18,000 millions, not counting deposits received from other UK banks. This cannot be directly compared with the estimate of the total size of the market, because of differences in the computation of the statistics. But London's role is plainly predominant. Within London, the American banks dominate the market, but they do not by any means monopolise it.

As stated in Part IID, banks in London may employ Euro-dollar deposits in four main ways; namely to lend out on the European inter-bank market, to lend to commercial customers (for periods from a few days to five years or more), to switch into sterling for employment in London's sterling money markets, and finally, in the case of US banks, to transfer back to head office in America. In December, 1971, almost £1,000 millions had been switched into sterling—in marked contrast to the position two years earlier when because of prolonged uncertainty about sterling and unfavourable interest rates on sterling investments,

* Bank of England, *Quarterly Economic Bulletin,* June, 1964.

very little was switched into sterling. About £8,000 millions was lent out to Western Europe, £2,500 millions to North America, £2,000 millions to overseas sterling countries and £1,300 millions to Latin America. Much of this lending was done by British banks and other (non-US) foreign banks in London; and this lending was often connected with the finance of trade, working capital for international companies and other commercial operations rather than purely money-market dealing.

Turning to the mechanism of the market, dealings in it are often arranged by foreign exchange brokers, commonly in units of $1 or $5 million or more. Deposits may be placed for periods ranging from call, up to two years or longer; most deposits are probably for periods between two days and three months. They may be renewed on maturity, at the then current interest rate.

Finally, let us list some of the ways in which the Euro-dollar market has influenced British banking:

It has enabled British banks to maintain their role in the financing of international trade and commerce at a time when the long decline of sterling would otherwise have seriously undermined their position. So a fair proportion of the world's trade continues to be financed through the City of London, even though the banks there have increasingly employed non-sterling currencies for the purpose.

It has encouraged American banks to open branches in London and facilitated the American economic penetration of Europe. This is perhaps the corollary, in the financial field, of the popular dictum that the only really European companies are the European subsidiaries of American companies.

Moreover, once American banks come to London, they inevitably look for opportunities in *sterling,* and in domestic business, as well as in dollar finance. So it has increased banking competition.

However, it has also encouraged the integration of Britain's money markets and banks with European banks. It has led directly to the formation of several co-operative ventures by British, French, Italian and German banks—and others.

It has stimulated the development of London's "new" money markets described above. It was probably only when bankers had learned that it was possible to lend millions of dollars by telephone on the strength of a bank's "name" (without other security) that they were bold enough to do the same thing domestically. The Euro-dollar market therefore also helped to create a whole new structure of interest rates in London, distinct from the traditional structure of rates in the discount market.

It has brought far more competition, especially for the clearing banks. The clearing banks still did not, until 1971-72, participate in the Euro-dollar market themselves significantly (only through subsidiaries). But the very rapid growth of the non-clearing banks is due partly to the Euro-dollar market.

The market seemed to open new sources of finance to British domestic borrowers. But the extent to which UK residents other than banks have been allowed to borrow foreign currencies depends markedly on official restrictions in force at the time—restrictions liable to sudden changes.

Indeed, by 1972 the major question hanging over the Euro-dollar market was the effect that governmental action, notably in Britain but also in other countries, would have. Increasingly governments were loth to let their domestic monetary policies be influenced or weakened by such external factors and bankers in London were pondering what new lending outlets they could find for their massive dollar deposits if they were to be barred from lending to European companies.

Dollar certificates of deposits

The negotiable dollar certificate of deposit was introduced to London in May, 1966, by the First National City Bank of New York; this type of instrument had already proved very successful in New York itself. Other banks in London (American, other foreign banks and British banks) were quick to follow the lead, and by 1970 many of them were issuing certificates. CDs yield about $\frac{1}{8}$ per cent less than the corresponding Euro-dollar maturity. In December, 1972, outstanding issues of dollar CDs totalled the equivalent of £3,400 millions. There is an active secondary market.

Indeed, the key to the attraction of CDs lies in an active and broadly-based secondary market. The merit of the certificate of deposit is that the holder can earn rates very little below those offered for a fixed-term deposit, but can still, if necessary, draw on the funds before the deposit matures, by negotiating (selling) the certificate in the market. The introduction of certificates of deposit has added to the facilities available for the investment of short-term funds in London.

Medium-term Euro-currency lending

International banks now recognize that they should be in a position to meet all the varied financial requirements of large international companies, particularly those operating in Europe. To be competitive, banks need not only good contacts and expert knowledge of potential customers' borrowing needs, but also the capacity to raise funds, of varying term, rapidly. Yet not many European banks are able to provide really large loans out of their own Euro-currency resources. For long-term money there is the Euro-bond market mentioned below. But, in the past four years, increasing interest has developed in the medium-term field, between one year and five or even ten years. In 1967-71 it suddenly became fashionable among banks to establish co-operative ventures (consortia) in this area, such as those listed in Table 19.

The Euro-bond market

Like the Euro-dollar market itself, the long-term Euro-bond market was stimulated by the financial needs of international companies, and by the US deficit which not only swelled the dollar holdings of Europeans and other people outside the United States but also caused the US administration to curb the freedom of US corporations in exporting funds from America, thus forcing them to borrow elsewhere. In the case of the Euro-bond market, the decisive turning point was the introduction of the Interest Equalization Tax in the United States in 1963 which in effect prevented foreign borrowers from raising long-term funds in New York, and thus exposed the inadequacies of European national capital markets. From small beginnings in the early 1960s, the volume of international bond issues rose to the equivalent of $1,000 millions in 1965 and to about $3,000 millions in 1968; and after a period of difficulty in 1968-69—when it was sometimes nearly impossible to float a new dollar loan because of the weakness of that currency—total issues rose to $3,600 millions in 1971. Most bonds issued are denominated in dollars or D-marks.

London banks faced many handicaps in such a market: first, the borrowers were at first mainly American companies or foreign governments; secondly, British residents can invest in such bonds only with "investment dollars" on which a premium has to be paid; third, the weakness of the UK balance of payments from 1964 to 1968 made sterling an unattractive currency in which to issue international bonds. Exchange control, currency instability and economic factors have all operated against their chances of playing a large role in this market. In their favour have been the expertise of some merchant banks in arranging issues for foreign borrowers over at least 100 years; and their contacts all over the world.

In the event, British banks and investment houses came to play an important role in two respects :

First, some leading merchant banks gained a prominent position as managers of new international issues, notably S. G. Warburg & Co., and N. M. Rothschild & Sons, mainly thanks to their ability to place bonds (i.e. raise funds) through contacts in Europe and elsewhere; some London-based American houses such as White Weld & Co., also play a prominent part in the primary issuing market.

Secondly, London is the main centre, with Brussels, for the trading of existing bonds : i.e. the secondary market. The principal houses are Strauss, Turnbull and Co., White Weld, Lloyds and Bolsa, Kidder Peabody and Western American Bank.

Part IV

Monetary Policy and The Bank of England

The subject of monetary policy can be analysed in a great number of different ways: it can be treated on a high theoretical level —there has been a great revival of academic interest in monetary policy in recent years; it can be analysed from an institutional point of view, (the role of the Bank of England, the commercial banks, the impact on the City of London, the sterling system, etc.); it can be described in terms of politics, contrasting Conservative and Labour Government policies, the influence of individual Chancellors of Exchequer, the political struggles that lie behind important decisions, such as devaluation in 1967; and so forth. Moreover, there is no agreement in England at present as to how important the whole subject is: some people regard monetary policy as the key to a successful overall economic policy; others still regard it as of little importance compared to fiscal policy (notably changes in taxation). So it is difficult to describe the subject fully; and impossible to do so briefly.

This outline will be confined to domestic monetary policy; it will adopt, broadly, an institutional approach, and it will seek to describe, first, the institutions concerned in the application of monetary policy, second, the aims of policy, and thirdly, the techniques.

THE INSTITUTIONS

The broad strategy of economic and monetary policy is decided by the Government in the Cabinet. The formulation of general economic policy is conducted by the Treasury, under the Chancellor of the Exchequer. The Bank of England is responsible for the implementation, co-ordination and application of the Government's monetary policy to other banks and financial institutions. It also retains great influence on wide policy decisions, and is represented on official committees through which economic policy is formulated and co-ordinated; it has a special responsibility in advising the Government on monetary affairs.

In starkest outline, that is the institutional framework of monetary policy in Britain. There are no special advisory agencies, or credit councils, as in other countries. In practice, it can be taken as a working assumption that most issues of monetary policy are effectively decided by the Treasury and the Bank of England. Naturally, they sometimes disagree with each other. In contrast to the position in other countries, such as the United States, such disputes are not usually fought out in the open, and the general public seldom becomes aware of them, although the Bank's views of the general economic situation and of particular issues are sometimes made public through the speeches of the Governor, and through the Bank's *Quarterly Economic Bulletin.* When the Bank was nationalized in 1946, the Treasury was granted formal powers to issue directions to the Bank, but this power has never been used. In the last resort, the Bank will defer to the Government; but the position of the Bank and its Governor, in the City and especially in international financial circles, is such that Governments will not lightly overrule its advice, especially when it is strongly felt.

The trouble is that it is nearly always difficult to find out what the Bank's views are, particularly on controversial issues. Journalists' or academics' reports that the Bank thinks such-and-such often have to be treated sceptically. But this is the fault of the still rather closeted way economic policy is discussed officially in Britain. Broadly speaking, the various Governors' speeches show that the Bank has tended to be in favour of the maximum degree of freedom, or *laissez-faire,* possible in the circumstances throughout the past 20 years; indeed, it is in some respects the most powerful repository of a "liberal" economic philosophy in England to-day. It was in favour of dismantling, as quickly as possible, the exchange controls and other restrictions built up during the 1930s and war years; it was in the forefront of the move to external convertibility in 1958; it has tried to retain, or go back to, a monetary policy implemented by action through the market (by open-market operations, etc.) rather than direct controls; it has consistently kept the door of the City open to foreign banks and generally favours competition in the City. Like other central banks, the Bank of England has been a stern critic of "excessive" Government expenditure, and has linked this with the need to avoid inflation. Another prominent preoccupation in the 1960s was the maintenance of confidence in the pound.

The Bank of England's relationship with the commercial banks is also ill-defined, and changing at the time of writing. The Bank of England Act, 1946, authorized the Bank to "request information from and make recommendations to bankers"; and, if so authorized by the Treasury, the Bank was granted the power to "issue directions to any banker for the purpose of securing that effect is given to any such request or recommendation". Here again, the power has never been used, though bankers are well aware that it exists.

In practice, the relationship has been founded on custom, convention and personal contact. The clearing banks have regular meetings with the Bank of England, and have in the past had a much closer relationship with it than other banks have. The Bank acts as the channel of communication between them and the Government. The clearing banks would not make any major move on matters of policy, certainly on matters affecting monetary policy, without informing the Bank; and the Bank would say whether it disapproved or not. The Bank, in its turn, represents the views of the banks to the Treasury. When the initiative for a certain policy comes from the Bank—as for instance in credit policy on bank lending—the usual practice has been for it to send letters to the banks "requesting" their co-operation in a certain direction; and it would probably, though not invariably, have consulted them beforehand in cases where they were expected actually to carry out the policy (as in the restriction of advances to certain categories of borrowers).

The importance of informal understandings and contacts has obvious advantages. It means that the Bank may be well informed about what is actually happening and being thought in the City. Unlike some other central banks, it has its roots deep in the financial structure and in the fast-moving, profit-oriented, commercial world around it. It means that the Bank, through its contacts and influence, may be able to act to forestall a commercial crisis (if, for example, some bank were getting into difficulties) before the crunch comes. It means that decisions can be put into effect quickly. And there is no doubt that the Bank's intimate knowledge of the City and its financial markets (it is in touch with the gilt-edged market and foreign exchange market every day, and operates in them frequently) is of great value to the Government. They also lend a special weight to the advice it gives to the Government.

But commentators have stressed disadvantages as well. Does not this kind of relationship, they ask, mean that matters can be left to drift? Since discussions between the Bank and the commercial banks (and, still more so, between the Bank and the Treasury) are, of course, held in private, there has seemed to be a lack of pressure on the parties concerned really to work out their own position.

Let us take, as an example, a question which much exercised the banks and their critics in the 1960s—whether the clearing banks should bid more actively for deposits. This question was raised, at the highest level, by the Governor of the Bank in a public speech in 1963—and was welcomed by many outside observers as a most constructive contribution to an important debate. But for years after that speech, it was well-nigh impossible to find out what the clearing banks themselves thought about this vital issue—apart from the fact that they did not much like it, and did not want to be disturbed. Previously, before 1963, the clearing banks had tended to say that it would not be worth their while to bid for deposits—that it would just raise the cost of their money without necessarily increasing the volume of deposits at their disposal; then, after the Governor's speech, they thought about it again, but said that the Chancellor (Mr. Maudling) had blocked it because it might raise interest rates; then they proceeded to set up special subsidiaries in order to do, in effect, what the Governor had suggested. But they remained confused over whether they wanted to bid *directly* themselves for deposits, rather than just through subsidiaries; neither the Treasury nor the Bank had publicly clarified its views on this vital issue, until the plain weaknesses of existing methods of credit control again brought the officials back to the drawing-board in 1969/70, and the new credit control system was introduced in 1971.

A similar confusion arose at the time of the bank mergers in 1967–68. Until then, it had been generally assumed in the City that the Bank of England was not in favour of further amalgamations among the big banks. Then, in 1967, an official inquiry into a separate issue (that of bank charges*) revealed that the authorities would not obstruct some further amalgamations—a strange way of clarifying official policy.

Another criticism sometimes raised by outsiders is that the

* National Board for Prices and Incomes, Report No. 34, Bank Charges, paragraph 154.

Bank's role as spokesman for the City may sometimes have inhibited it from forming a separate judgment of its own, as Britain's central bank, on great issues of policy. Indeed, may not its duties come into conflict, albeit semi-consciously? On this view, it might be better if the City had a separate body to represent it in Whitehall, and lobby the Government, thus leaving the Bank more free to concentrate on matters of policy. On the other hand, there might then be a risk of weakening the Bank's intimate links with the City.

THE AIMS OF MONETARY POLICY

The aims of monetary policy during the past 20 years have been those of economic policy generally, shared broadly throughout the western world, i.e. the maintenance of full employment and the encouragement of economic growth whilst restraining inflation and preserving equilibrium in the balance of payments. It is easily said; and if policy has failed to achieve these aims —and it has failed—it is a failure only in some respects. It has failed in the sense that Britain's economic growth rate during these years has lagged behind that of many other countries. It has also failed in that some of the problems that Britain faced at the beginning of the period—external payments difficulties, excessive short-term liabilities overseas, and internal inflation—were still in evidence at the end of the period. But it has succeeded by historical standards, in that Britain's economic growth during the past generation has probably been greater than in any previous time—though it is not clear how much, if any, of the credit for that should go to economic policy. And there has been a further item which many people would place on the credit side; despite the lurch to direct controls in 1964–69, the country retained an essentially free economy.

The broad aim of domestic monetary policy, therefore, together with fiscal policy, has been to influence the trend of aggregate demand in the economy (so as to achieve the ultimate aims mentioned above). On this, there is general agreement. But the next question is, what is the precise monetary measure that the authorities should seek to influence? This amounts to much the same thing as asking, how can one tell that monetary policy is being effective? Which variable should be watched and influenced? There is still no general agreement on the answer.

The Radcliffe Committee, which reported in 1959 and remains a central source of information and opinion on the monetary system, thought that there were two main channels through which the monetary authorities could influence demand. In the first place, there were *interest rates,* particularly the long-term rate of interest, which could directly affect business investment and other components of demand, such as housebuilding; the Committee strongly recommended that the authorities should take a view on the appropriate structure of interest rates and seize the opportunities presented to them by the size of the national debt, and their management of it, to bring about that desirable structure of rates. Secondly, the Committee emphasised the importance of influencing the *general liquidity* of the economy, and especially of financial institutions; "spending is not limited by the amount of money in existence; but it is related to the amount people think they can get hold of, whether by receipts of income . . . disposal of capital assets or borrowing". The market for credit, the Committee stressed, was a single market, and the monetary authorities should seek to influence all the sources of credit. They should not concentrate on only one, such as the supply of money. This linked up with the first point (on interest rates) for it was precisely through resolute action on interest rates and on the relationship between long- and short-term rates, that the authorities could (in the Committee's view) change the liquidity of financial operators throughout the country, and therefore their willingness to lend money to customers.

In short, the Radcliffe Committee thought that the monetary authorities should adopt a more positive approach in their open market operations in Government securities, and that the aim of such a policy should be to affect the liquidity of the whole economy as well as the cash reserves (or the liquidity base) of the deposit banks themselves. The importance of the clearing banks was that they were the biggest lenders in the financial system; and not so much in any unique function as "creators of money". The Committee tended to play down the importance of the money supply in itself. Many people—including the monetary authorities—have been sympathetic in principle to the broad philosophy of the Radcliffe Report.

However, the concept of "general liquidity" was not one that could be easily measured. The aim of policy has all too often been to restrain domestic demand. In actual practice, as we shall see, the authorities have, until recently, relied very heavily on *ad hoc* expedients: namely, on *direct controls on the lending* of the particular financial institutions—mainly banks and finance companies. Everybody agreed that such direct controls had many disadvantages; they tended to bear unfairly on the institutions concerned, and to distort the whole development of the financial institutions; they were a brake on efficiency; above all, they were arbitrary in their effect and *ineffective,* in the long run. This was partly because they encouraged the growth of "fringe" operations outside the scope of official controls but mainly because, in their concentration on the volume of lending, the authorities allowed the volume of bank *deposits* and other "near money" *liquid resources* to grow very rapidly. This is exactly what happened in the mid-1960s; growth in the money supply accelerated sharply in the years 1965-67, although bank *advances* came under strict control, and although economic policy was supposed to be restrictive. This meant that many companies and individuals found little difficulty in financing a continued increase in their expenditure even though they were prevented from borrowing money from places like the banks. It was increasingly realised that this rapid growth in the money supply and in the liquidity of the economy was severely undermining the Government's efforts to curb demand.

Thus, gradually there came about a great revival of attention on monetary policy, and in particular on the money supply itself. Two other developments contributed to this: first, the International Monetary Fund (then Britain's biggest creditor) pressed the British Government to pay more attention to the growth of the money supply; secondly, the "monetary school" of academic economists launched a determined, and well-argued, campaign to support their view that money supply itself does matter. To appreciate the impact of this, it must be remembered that in England, the practical effect of Lord Keynes' teaching had been to focus attention on taxation and fiscal policy (whether Lord Keynes himself ever intended this is another matter).

About this time, a general monetary indicator was developed by the authorities called "Domestic Credit Expansion". This is defined as the increase in the money supply *plus* the external deficit (or *less* the external surplus) in the balance of payments. The money supply is defined as the deposits (both current deposits and time deposits) of UK residents with banks in the UK (deposit banks and "wholesale" banks) *plus* notes and coin (cash) in the hands of the public. The external deficit for these purposes is defined as the Government's net borrowing from overseas (or the net reduction in the foreign exchange reserves and other assets) and the overseas borrowing of public corporations and local authorities.

The reason for developing this new measure, in preference to the money supply itself, was explained by the Bank of England as follows:

> "In the case of an open economy, particularly one as dependent on foreign trade as the United Kingdom's, internal inflationary pressure will, to some considerable extent, spill over from the domestic economy into increased expenditure abroad. Under such circumstances, the internal rates of growth of money incomes and prices, and the associated rise in the money supply, will tend to be diminished and will thus become less useful as indicators of internal inflationary pressures. In this respect D.C.E. seems to be a more satisfactory indicator, since it measures the main factors leading to an expansion in the money supply, whether or not such expansion is cut back subsequently by the use of such money balances for the purpose of making expenditures abroad."*

If this indicator had been available in the mid-1960s and if the authorities had paid attention to it, a genuinely restrictive monetary policy might have been adopted long before it was. Thus, in 1964, when the UK plunged into external deficit, and inflationary pressures were mounting, the money supply (on the usual definition) was not rising much faster than in the previous period of economic boom, in 1959; but the domestic credit expansion was accelerating at an unparallelled rate. In that year, the DCE amounted to about £1,500 millions whereas the money supply itself rose by only £600 millions. In the five years 1964-68, when economic policy was generally supposed to be restrictive, the domestic credit expansion totalled £5,300 millions, far more than in the whole of the previous 12 years from 1952 to 1963. It is hardly surprising, in view of these figures, that the Government found it impossible in those years to control inflation or demand by raising taxes. In 1969-71, the fashion swung back to the money stock itself (bank deposits and cash) as the UK moved into payments surplus and efforts were directed at stimulating economic activity—but there was also a tendency to play down the importance of money.

* Bank of England, *Quarterly Economic Bulletin,* September 1969.

TECHNIQUES OF MONETARY POLICY

The next question is, how have the authorities conducted monctary policy? The answer falls naturally into two parts: for 1971 marked a watershed—or at least a determined bid to adopt a new tack. Before 1971, the authorities had relied for a generation on direct controls on bank lending (which is only one of the dynamic elements in the money supply), by requests to the banks. After 1971 they changed, and decided to focus on the whole stock of money.

Direct controls on banks

The following quotation from the Bank of England's *Quarterly Bulletin* for June, 1969, put the case for direct controls, and at the same time recognized some of their disadvantages:

> "One of the difficulties that has confronted the authorities in their efforts to further national economic policy through control of the banking sector is that restraint of bank lending has often seemed appropriate at times when it has been difficult to sell large quantities of government debt to the private sector. The consequent reliance on the banking sector for residual borrowing generates the liquidity with which the banks could frustrate official objectives. Particularly in some of the carlier years of this period, the banks had such large holdings of liquid assets that, even when conditions allowed for large sales of debt to the public, it was hardly possible to put severe pressure on their liquidity position. Such excess liquidity can be sterilised by requesting the banks to place Special Deposits with the Bank of England, which are not counted as liquid assets for the purpose of meeting the required ratio. The same object —the restriction of bank lending to the private sector—can, however, be achieved with greater simplicity by the use of direct controls. Such direct controls can be used flexibly, for example to indicate priorities in lending to which it might be desirable for the banks to adhere. Direct controls, unlike calls for Special Deposits, leave the banks free to manage their holdings of government debt as they see fit. In the longer run, however, it is recognised that distortions of the structure and efficiency of the banking sector may result."*

* The UK Banking Sector, 1951-67, in *Quarterly Economic Bulletin,* June 1969.

Direct "requests" (or in other words controls) to the banks to restrain their lending were made at various times throughout the period from 1950 to 1970. During this time, there were two main developments in these "requests": first, they embraced a wider and wider circle of financial institutions; secondly, they became more and more specific and detailed.

During the 1950s, the requests were confined to the deposit banks. In 1951, for instance, the banks were asked to restrict credit to essential requirements; then, in 1955, the banks were asked to make a "positive and significant reduction" in their advances over the next few months (interpreted as a 10 per cent reduction); in 1957, they were asked to keep the level of their advances for the following year to the average of the previous 12 months. Then, in 1958, all restrictions were lifted.

They were reimposed in 1960 and tightened in 1961; but it was no longer possible, on grounds of either equity or efficiency, to restrict the ceilings to deposit banks alone, and on this occasion the request was addressed to all groups of banks and to a wide range of financial institutions. The terms of the request, however, remained fully general. The restrictions were lifted in the autumn of 1962.

When lending ceilings were reimposed in 1965 and tightened in 1966 they were much more specific; all banks (not only the deposit banks) and the hire purchase finance houses were asked to restrict their lending to an annual rate of increase of 5 per cent in the 12 months to March, 1966, and the quantitative request was accompanied by detailed qualitative guidance on the various categories of borrowers that should receive high or low priority. In 1966, also, the controls were extended to cover commercial bills and acceptances. Such quantitative controls, modified slightly, continued into 1971, when they were gradually dissolved as economic policy became, for a time, expansionary.

Controls on hire purchase transactions

An even more specific form of control was directed at hire purchase transactions; here, the authorities frequently changed, by order, both the maximum "repayment" period allowed (say, to two years instead of three) and the minimum deposit that customers are required to put down, in cash. These controls on the terms of hire purchase transactions had a powerful impact on consumer credit extended through finance houses for the purchase of cars and consumer durable goods. Hire purchase controls were used quite actively in the 1950s and 1960s; indeed, the terms were changed 13 times between 1959 and 1970. There was, however, persistent criticism of this weapon, not only because it hit directly at Britain's motor car industry, but also because it was discriminating and increasingly avoided.

THE NEW MONETARY POLICY

Thus past critics of British banking, as well as the City of London itself, joined in the applause for the final launching in September, 1971, of Britain's new banking and credit policy.* Ever since the Bank of England had released its proposals the previous May for the reform of the conventions governing banking in Britain, and for lifting of all direct official intervention in bank activities, there had been an air of impending liberation in the City. As soon as the reforms were in effect, and banks engaged in open and equal combat for customers and deposits, nobody seemed to doubt that their labours would engender vast changes in their outlook, their services and structure, and even their role in society. The City became full of talk about how the big banks would be going all out for new types of business as competition pushed up the cost of their funds; how they would have to cut costs, prune expensive branch networks, develop new types of expertise, and how other banks and financial institutions would respond. Yet the City was also well aware that this new freedom sprang from the authorities' embrace of a different type of monetary policy—a policy which would work through market forces, and not by direct controls on bank credit. If the policy worked in practice, there would be a massive two-fold gain to society (more efficient banking and a better monetary policy). If it failed, the banks could be saddled with more controls than ever before.

This new approach in fact represented a new official bid to return in practice to something like the old orthodox textbook system. Under it, the Bank intends to control the money supply through generating or syphoning off funds in the system, thus lowering or raising interest rates (including bank lending rates) and so stimulating or choking off the demand for bank credit. Each of these is considered in turn.

* This appraisal of the new monetary policy is based on an article by the author in *The Banker,* October 1971.

The objective

The central aim of the policy, which is still at the time of revision (autumn, 1972) in its early stages, is to control the rate of growth of the money stock. Ignoring the technicalities, this measures the amount of money that people, companies, etc. have in their pockets or at the banks; and so influences their spending, the rate of inflation and employment. Naturally, it had long been regarded as one of the more important things a central bank can try to control. But in Britain, as explained already, it had often grown quickly just at those times when it should have been held back. This was partly because the Bank of England had been trying to do many other (partly incompatible) things as well, such as holding down interest rates or pushing bank lending in certain directions; partly because, even in a squeeze, interest rates were not free to respond fully to supply and demand; and partly because, under the old rules, the clearing banks could have circumvented a squeeze on their liquid assets (by, for example, channelling loan demand into commercial bills, until this was stopped by direct "request"). Knowing this, the authorities seldom tried to exert a proper conventional squeeze on bank liquidity.

As a result, as already explained, the authorities had for 20 years tried to influence expenditure by direct controls on bank advances, rather than deposits (i.e. crudely the amount people can borrow rather than the amount they own). The Governor himself pronounced the epitaph to that era, when, after recalling some apparent attractions of the system, he declared to the world's bankers at Munich in May, 1971 :

> "We must beware of believing that if we do succeed in restraining bank lending we have necessarily and to the same extent been operating a restrictive credit policy. We may by our very actions stimulate the provision of credit through non-bank channels; we may introduce distortions into the financial system; and we may indeed be distorting in harmful ways the deployment of the real resources of the country."

Setting interest rates free

The growth of the money supply in any period is governed mainly by the increase in bank lending to the private sector, and the increase in Government borrowing from the banks (ignoring for the moment any inflow or outflow of funds from abroad). Both processes create bank deposits : lending puts more funds into the hands of the public, while official borrowing from the banks implies that the excess of Government expenditure in any period over Government revenue (from taxation, etc.) is not offset by greater public investment in Government securities (national savings, gilt-edged, etc.) but is instead being held on deposit at the banks. The only way to keep the money supply under control is therefore to limit these expansionary influences. This can be done by compulsion—ordering the banks to stop lending, and ordering (as in war time) the public to invest in Government securities.

But in a free system, the only way to accomplish it is, (a) to make the yield on Government securities so attractive that the public wants to invest in them and, (b) to allow interest rates on bank lending to rise until only the most worthy borrowers can pay them, i.e. those whose activities are so profitable that they can afford to pay. Both require that interest rates throughout the system should be free rapidly to adjust to changes in the supply and demand for funds, and that the authorities themselves should be willing to let them rise to their free market level.

These conditions did not exist previously. To create them, three steps were taken. First, all conventions linking commercial bank lending and deposit rates to other rates (i.e. Bank Rate) were removed; second, all such conventions in the money market, and the practice whereby the discount houses made a collective agreed bid at the weekly Treasury bill auction, were also abolished; third, the authorities formally put an end to the convention whereby they had always been willing, at a price, to buy back long-term Government securities—a practice which had had the effect of keeping up bond prices above, and interest rates below, the free market level. As announced in May, 1971, they are no longer prepared to buy outright government stock maturing in more than one year's time.

From October, 1971, therefore, the clearing banks had to declare what rates they, individually, would be offering for deposits and charging on loans. On lending rates, they have adopted a "base rate" system whereby each bank sets its own basic rate, with customers being charged various rates at increasing margins above it. But the important thing is that this rate itself now changes not with Bank Rate, but with changes in the banks' own views of the most profitable rate. Since all 200 banks will be competing for custom, the chances of any back door "understanding" on rates is small.

The rules

In addition to freeing interest rates, the authorities armed themselves with two other, rather more debatable, weapons:

1. The new reserve asset ratio: all banks have to keep a minimum of $12\frac{1}{2}$ per cent of their "eligible liabilities" in certain reserve assets—Treasury bills, commercial bills, Government securities with less than a year to run to maturity and call money with the London money market. Finance houses have to keep 10 per cent. This replaced the previous liquidity ratio and is applied to all banks, not just the big deposit banks.

2. Special Deposits: they will also, on occasion, tell banks to place another slice of their assets in a frozen account with the Bank of England (which, however, bears interest at a rate close to the going Treasury bill rate).

The new reserve asset ratio was welcome in that it put all banks on an equal footing; previously, the Bank of England tended to argue that the differences between the 200-odd banks in London were so great that no uniform rules could be devised to apply to all of them, and rightly considered that different ratios for different types of banks would introduce still more distortions into the system. By emphasizing the similarities of the sterling business of the banks, and giving foreign banks, etc., time to come into line, the Bank decided it could manage with only one ratio. Rightly it also resisted any temptation to put different reserve requirements on different types of business. Calls for special deposits would also be uniform across the banking system; the only provision being that different rates of call might be made for overseas deposits.

However, some would argue that there is no need for reserve ratios at all, or special deposits—that the authorities can control the money stock simply by their operations in the markets, and interest rates. All that is required is a small cash ratio—if that. Making the banks hold any particular set of reserves involves some distortion in market forces—interest rates on the investments that qualify for reserve assets will probably be lower than they would be in a totally free system. This case is hard to fault in theory, but is simply not acceptable to the Bank of England, or probably to any other central bank, at present. It feels now, at least, that it has ensured some reliable demand for Government debt, and a firm principle on which to operate. But it needs to be on its guard against using such requirements blatantly to channel bank funds into Government hands and, in particular, against using special deposits as a substitute for market methods and interest rates action.

THE POLICY IN PRACTICE

Such are the bare bones of the "new" policy. How should it work in practice?

To begin with, the authorities must choose what rate of growth of the money stock they wish to allow in the period ahead. This "target" is already an important element in the Government's economic policy, and will be worked out in greater detail in future. It should certainly be published—the Chancellor said in presenting the 1972 Budget that he was not seeking "immediately to reduce the growth of money supply to much below 3 per cent a quarter"—together, one hopes, with the reasons for the choice made.

They must then take a view of the likely expansion of bank lending to the private sector, which will depend on the financial position of the various sectors of the economy, the room that banks have to finance such an expansion (without falling below the $12\frac{1}{2}$ per cent reserve requirement) and the likely course of economic activity. They will also have available to them estimates of the likely deficit in the Government's finances (i.e. its borrowing requirement) and the proportion of this that might be covered by higher national savings, higher holdings of notes and coin, etc. This net deficit will tell them the amount they have to raise in the market, unless they positively want to generate additional deposits on top of that created by the growth of bank lending.

This exercise can have some rather horrifying results. All too often, it may end by suggesting that the money supply is likely to grow far too fast, and in the first half of 1972, it was indeed growing at an unprecedented rate of 25 per cent per annum.

The system allows three main methods of curbing the potential money growth.

Special deposits: These would be used to head off a possible big upsurge in bank lending, at times when the banks had significant "excess reserves" (above their $12\frac{1}{2}$ per cent minimum). The Bank, however, is very anxious not to use this weapon too much, for fear of slipping back into direct regulation. Moreover, it only freezes a proportion of bank assets—it cannot exert a cumulative pressure on bank reserve assets. It would, however, tend to push up short-term money rates, as banks sought to rebuild their excess reserves, and it would also be a warning that the Bank was shifting to a more restrictive policy.

Money market operations: As the dominant operator in the market, the Bank could push short-term rates up, either by forcing the discount houses to last resort loans at a penal rate (and the Bank intends to make sure that the market comes to it only as a last resort), or through the prices at which it deals from day to day in Treasury bills.

Sales of Government securities: As mentioned, this is the main method of raising long-term finance for the Government, and squeezing the cash base of the banks and their reserve assets. It is particularly important that the authorities make clear that they will not help banks to move out of gilt-edged (when, for instance, they want to replenish their reserve assets); since the market would weaken sharply as soon as it anticipated big selling by banks, the banks would face the prospect of taking sharp realized losses on their sales, if they wanted to increase their reserve assets and so continue to expand their loans and deposits. At the same time, such a fall in bond prices and rise in interest rates would lift rates throughout the system and (now there is a free market) also the costs of bank funds, squeezing their profit margins. There would thus be a large, increasing pressure on them to raise their lending rates or curb their advances.

WILL IT WORK?

The Treasury and Bank were therefore plainly determined to get right away from direct interference in banking and to make the new system work. But there were still several hidden reefs to be negotiated. Very briefly, a few of them were:

1. The threat to building societies, savings banks and the national savings movement. If a real struggle developed for "small" savings, and funds threatened to be pulled from building societies, etc., there might be awkward political trouble. However, the tax advantages enjoyed by depositors in these institutions made this still a medium-term worry.

2. Overseas funds; a squeeze exerted through interest rates would tend to pull in overseas money, against the aims of policy. This can be a problem for all advanced countries with open financial systems, and may be met partly by concerted action between Governments. In addition, special deposits (perhaps up to 100 per cent) might be imposed on overseas funds coming into

the banking system; or a special tax levied; or exchange control imposed.

3. Personal lending: the Bank reserved the right to issue some "guidance" on bank lending, especially personal lending. This would sully the purity of the scheme. But given the political will, such a move would probably not be used as a screen to reintroduce more wide-ranging controls.

4. Treasury bills: at first sight, it seemed as if the banks might be able to evade a squeeze on their assets by bidding Treasury bills and other reserve assets away from non-bank holders; this would push up interest rates, but might it delay an intended official squeeze?

5. The big test would, it seemed, come over interest rates; if they did threaten to rise far above any previous experience, in a future tight-money exercise, would the political will hold? There was the related problem of the speed with which Governments like to act in a "crisis". Such crises have often seemed to take Governments by surprise, the pressure for some sudden gesture builds up quickly. In the past, however, this pressure has usually sprung from balance of payments fears—of a flight from sterling. This is where the new credit scheme links up with the greater flexibility on exchange rates. If flexibility on both is upheld, there seems a chance of avoiding precipitate action in future. Experience during the first year of operation of the new policy, in 1972, suggested that the authorities were still reluctant to accept the necessary degree of flexibility—not indeed on the exchanges, where sterling was floated—but in interest rates.

APPENDIX: THE NEW CREDIT CONTROLS DEFINED

The following information comes from an official announcement about the new credit controls:

Eligible liabilities, against which the reserve assets have to be held, are defined as the sterling deposit liabilities of the banking system as a whole, excluding deposits having an original maturity of over two years, plus any sterling resources obtained by switching foreign currencies into sterling. Inter-bank transactions and sterling certificates of deposit (both held and issued) are taken into the calculation of individual banks' liabilities on a net basis, irrespective of term. Adjustments are made in respect of transit items.

Eligible reserve assets comprise balances with the Bank of England (other than Special Deposits), British Government and

Northern Ireland Government Treasury bills, company tax reserve certificates, money at call with the London money market, British Government stocks with one year or less to final maturity, local authority bills eligible for rediscount at the Bank of England and (up to a maximum of 2 per cent of eligible liabilities) commercial bills eligible for rediscount at the Bank of England.

Eligible money at call with the London money market comprise funds placed with members of the London Discount Market Association, with certain other firms carrying on an essentially similar type of business (the discount brokers and the money trading departments of certain banks traditionally undertaking such business) and with certain firms through whom the banks finance the gilt-edged market, namely the money brokers and jobbers. In order to constitute an eligible reserve asset, funds placed with these firms must be at call (or callable, if not explicitly at call) and must be secured (in the case of the jobbers, on gilt-edged securities).

Special deposits, when called, will be a uniform percentage across the banking system, normally of each bank's total eligible liabilities; further consideration will be given to the possibility of different rates of call relating to overseas deposits. Calls and repayments will normally be announced on a Thursday with the announcement of Bank Rate. Amounts called will be rounded to the nearest £5,000 and will be adjusted monthly to take account of changes in eligible liabilities as reported to the Bank. Special Deposits will bear interest at a rate equivalent to the Treasury bill rate.

Interest rates. The London and Scottish clearing banks will abandon their collective agreements on interest rates as part of the new arrangements. In the light of discussions held with the banks, the authorities see no need, at least in present circumstances, to seek to limit the terms offered by the banks for savings deposits to protect the position of the savings banks and building societies.

Transitional arrangements. Firstly, after allowing for the repayment of existing Special Deposits it was apparent that the reserve asset holdings of the London clearing banks over and above the prescribed minimum level would be quite out of proportion to their present and immediately prospective level of lending. These banks have therefore agreed to subscribe for some £750 millions of three new government stocks, maturing respectively two, three and six years hence, to be issued concurrently with the repayment of outstanding Special Deposits. Secondly, individual banks whose holdings of reserve assets have hitherto been well below the prescribed ratio have been given the opportunity of agreeing with the Bank appropriate transitional periods (not extending beyond the end of the year) during which their reserve asset holdings may be built up gradually to the prescribed level.

The money market. Agreement was reached with the London Discount Market Association on the basis of the Bank's proposals for the market published in July, 1971. Members of the Association continue to apply each week for a total amount of Treasury bills, sufficient to cover the amount of bills offered at the tender. They also maintain at least 50 per cent of their funds in defined categories of public sector debt. The Association informed the Bank that, from the introduction of the new arrangements, they would no longer tender for Treasury bills at an agreed price. The discount brokers outside the Association continue to participate in the Treasury bill tender and maintain a similar minimum ratio of public sector debts, as do the money trading departments of certain banks (which will be treated separately from the rest of their business for this purpose). The Bank continues to confine to the money market access to last resort lending facilities.

The categories of public sector debt to be included in the ratio will be British Government and Northern Ireland Government Treasury bills, company tax reserve certificates, local authority bills and bonds, and British Government, British Government-guaranteed and local authority stocks with not more than five years to run to maturity.

Finance houses. Agreement was reached with members of the Finance Houses Association (and with certain individual houses outside the Association) on a scheme parallel to that agreed with the banks.

In all essentials the scheme for finance houses closely follows that for the banks. Eligible liabilities, as for the banks, exclude deposits having an original maturity of over two years; however, as the houses remain outside the banking system amounts borrowed from banks are excluded, so that the liability to hold reserve assets and make Special Deposits is not applied twice to the same funds. The required minimum reserve asset ratio will be 10 per cent instead of $12\frac{1}{2}$ per cent, but the definition of eligible reserve assets is the same.

Appendix: Tables

Table 1. Deposit-taking Institutions 1971

Deposits: £ millions

		Total		UK residents
BANKING SECTOR				
Deposit banks		14,547		13,538
"Wholesale" banks		22,852		3,005
Discount market		398		347
National Giro		75		75
	Total	**37,872**	**Total**	**16,965**
OTHER INSTITUTIONS				
Building Societies*		12,176		12,176
Savings Banks†		2,654		2,654
Finance companies		823		760
	Total (approx.)	**15,653**	**Total**	**15,590**

*Shares and deposits.
†Deposits at "ordinary accounts" of National Savings Bank and "ordinary department" of Trustee Savings Banks, March 1972.

Table 2. Deposits and Advances by Sector (to ends of periods)

(£ millions)

	Total	Total UK residents	UK residents: UK public sector	UK residents: Companies and financial institutions	UK residents: Other private sector	Overseas residents
Total Deposits						
1965	14,725	10,865	394	3,269	7,202	3,860
1969	27,493	13,959	457	4,262	9,240	13,358
1971	37,872	16,965	524	5,410	11,031	20,203
Deposit banks						
1965	10,080	9,651	389	2,349	6,913	429
1969	11,789	11,330	387	2,335	8,608	459
1971	14,547	13,538	434	2,869	10,235	928
"Wholesale" banks						
1965	4,534	1,137	5	867	265	3,397
1969	15,559	2,500	44	1,852	604	12,883
1971	22,852	3,005	49	2,255	701	19,224
Discount market						
1965	111	77	—	53	24	34
1969	109	93	—	71	22	16
1971	398	347	—	278	69	51
Total Advances						
1965	9,184	6,897	786	4,213	1,898	2,287
1969	21,179	9,121	1,637	5,588	1,896	12,058
1971	29,428	12,596	2,549	7,492	2,555	16,832
Deposit banks						
1965	5,392	5,269	214	3,269	1,786	123
1969	6,326	5,877	268	3,856	1,753	449
1971	7,619	6,878	412	4,141	2,325	741
"Wholesale" banks						
1965	3,776	1,612	566	940	106	2,164
1969	14,809	3,200	1,349	1,709	142	11,609
1971	21,713	5,622	2,092	3,303	227	16,091
Discount market						
1965	16	16	6	4	6	—
1969	28	28	4	23	1	—
1971	85	85	34	48	3	—

These figures exclude transactions confined within the UK banking sector. Thus they reflect broadly the banking sector's transactions with the rest of the economy. The figures given under "Total" also include the National Giro (with deposits of £75 millions in 1971) and sterling certificates of deposit (totalling £704 millions). "Wholesale" banks comprise the merchant banks, British overseas and Commonwealth banks, foreign banks and other banks.

Table 3. Bank Lending Margins

Type of customer	Rate charged	Notes
Nationalised industries (with Treasury guarantee)	$\frac{1}{2}$ per cent over syndicate base rate* with minimum $4\frac{1}{2}$ per cent	Some lending is at 1 per cent over syndicate base rate, reflecting the use of funds advanced in hire purchase business.
Local authorities Building Societies Insurance companies Other first class industrial and commercial borrowers	Base rate + 1 per cent with minimum 5 per cent	
Export loans (guaranteed by ECGD)	(i) Minimum lending rate, minimum $4\frac{1}{2}$ per cent	For loans up to 2 years.
	(ii) Fixed rate of 6 per cent to borrower	For loans for 2–15 years (subject to 1 per cent commitment fee to cover whole term).
Other industrial and commercial borrowers and all private customers	At discretion	Normally 1 per cent to 4 per cent above the bank's "base rate".

*Base rates are fixed by each bank independently; they may differ from bank to bank, although they are normally at the same level. Lending rates are settled by reference to base rate. Where banks operate as a consortium, a "common" or "syndicate" base rate is fixed.

Table 4. London Clearing Banks – Main Balance Sheet Items

1. Deposits 1955–72

(£ millions)

End-year or mid-December*	Current accounts	Deposit accounts	Other accounts	Total gross deposits	"Net" deposits†
1951	4,221	1,839	273	6,333	5,945
1952	4,169	2,016	275	6,460	6,056
1953	4,247	2,105	342	6,694	6,256
1954	4,403	2,144	394	6,941	6,421
1955	4,251	2,000	361	6,612	6,137
1956	4,187	2,054	416	6,656	6,209
1957	4,107	2,377	445	6,929	6,390
1958	4,227	2,486	486	7,199	6,618
1959	4,417	2,507	515	7,439	6,902
1960	4,296	2,588	639	7,523	8,901
1961	4,166	2,711	678	7,555	7,018
1962	4,385	2,783	735	7,903	7,309
1963	4,795	2,814	728	8,337	7,721
1964	4,986	3,079	931	8,996	8,226
1965	5,019	3,458	976	9,454	8,652
1966	4,905	3,628	969	9,501	8,760
1967	5,298	3,963	1,001	10,262	9,412
1968	5,487	4,273	976	10,736	9,898
1969	5,350	4,361	1,013	10,724	9,801
1970§	5,678	4,619	309	10,606	9,997
1971	6,625	5,576	356	12,557	11,859
1972 (June)	6,941	6,867	443	14,251	13,514

*End-December to 1958; thereafter at the mid-December make-up date.
†Excluding cheques in course of collection on other banks in the UK and items in transit between offices of the same bank.
§Figures, notably for "other accounts", affected by the banks' decision to reveal their true profits and reserves and other accounting changes which reduced gross deposits by some £800 millions in January 1970.

Table 4. London Clearing Banks – Main Balance Sheet Items

2. Liquid Assets 1951–72

(£ millions)

End-year or mid-Dec.	Coin, notes and balances with the Bank of England	Money at call and short notice	Treasury bills	Commercial bills	Other bills	Total liquid assets	Per cent of deposits (the liquidity ratio)
1951	531	598	791	181	—	2,100	**33.2**
1952	550	529	1,182	66	—	2,327	**36.0**
1953	542	501	1,338	79	—	2,460	**36.7**
1954	571	498	1,199	114	—	2,382	**34.3**
1955	565	506	1,271	129	—	2,471	**37.4**
1956	571	505	1,275	140	—	2,492	**37.4**
1957	601	525	1,403	135	—	2,664	**38.4**
1958	586	587	1,185	135	—	2,493	**34.6**
1959	600	560	1,218	141	23	2,542	**34.2**
1960	615	623	1,006	133	22	2,399	**31.9**
1961	626	706	1,081	195	57	2,665	**35.3**
1962	644	786	986	197	71	2,684	**34.0**
1963	690	787	940	231	74	2,723	**32.7**
1964	767	882	679	343	83	2,754	**30.6**
1965	792	1,020	770	356	100	3,039	**32.1**
1966	800	1,171	681	354	120	3,126	**32.9**
1967	822	1,366	450	347	142	3,127	**30.5**
1968	865	1,487	510	302	223	3,385	**31.5**
1969	894	1,549	394	258	350	3,445	**32.1**
1970	830	1,590	406	305	459	3,590	**33.8**
1971	808	1,504	199	568	535	3,614	**28.8**
1972 (June)	834	1,323	120	525	23†	2,825	**19.8**

†Affected by the decision to include re-financeable export credits in advances.

Note: After September 1971 the liquidity ratio lost the significance it had formerly held since, for purposes of monetary policy, it was replaced by a reserve asset ratio, as explained in the text.

Table 4. London Clearing Banks – Main Balance Sheet Items

3. Other Assets – "Risk" Assets (£ millions)

	Investments			Advances to customers and other accounts†		
End or mid-Dec.*	Total	% of deposits	of which British Government stocks	Total	% of deposits	Other than to nationalized industries
1951	2,067	**32.6**	1,990	1,860	**29.4**	1,771
1952	2,148	**33.3**	2,076	1,665	**25.8**	1,558
1953	2,275	**34.0**	2,194	1,611	**24.1**	1,551
1954	2,353	**33.9**	2,261	1,783	**25.7**	1,661
1955	2,016	**30.5**	1,928	1,747	**26.4**	1,715
1956	1,980	**29.8**	1,893	1,832	**27.5**	1,723
1957	2,049	**29.6**	1,962	1,777	**25.7**	1,698
1958	2,102	**29.2**	1,994	2,126	**29.5**	2,046
1959	1,720	**23.1**	1,597	2,795	**37.6**	2,713
1960	1,288	**17.1**	1,159	3,229	**42.9**	3,159
1961	1,119	**14.8**	1,007	3,209	**42.5**	3,141
1962	1,315	**16.6**	1,204	3,506	**44.4**	3,435
1963	1,281	**15.4**	1,163	3,961	**47.5**	3,897
1964	1,179	**13.1**	1,056	4,538	**50.4**	4,464
1965	1,185	**12.5**	1,047	4,569	**48.3**	4,512
1966	1,181	**12.4**	1,040	4,492	**47.3**	4,425
1967	1,405	**13.7**	1,252	4,862	**47.4**	4,698
1968	1,432	**13.3**	1,266	5,039	**46.9**	4,968
1969	1,105	**10.3**	931	5,194	**48.4**	5,123
1970	1,062	**10.0**	873	5,597	**54.8**	5,495
1971	2,003	**16.0**	1,823	6,831	**56.1**	6,679
1972 (June)	1,638	**11.5**	1,436	9,735	**70.1**	9,609

*End-December to 1958; thereafter the mid-December make-up date.

†Total advances are shown net of transit items.

Table 5. European Banking Groups

Participating banks	Partners' total assets*	Year started	Group co-ordinating company	Joint overseas ventures	Comments
Amsterdam-Rotterdam Bank Creditanstalt Bankverein Deutsche Bank Midland Bank Société Générale Société Générale de Banque Banca Commerciale Italiana joined in 1973	50,907	1963	European Banks International Company (EBIC)	European-American Banks (New York); representative offices in Johannesburg, Djakarta, Toronto, European-Asiatic Bank, Hamburg; and, with other partners, Banque Européenne de Crédit à Moyen Terme (Brussels) and Euro-Pacific Finance Corp (Melbourne). Also joint company with Arab banks in Luxembourg (branches in Brussels and Hamburg)	Société Générale and Creditanstalt Bankverein joined in 1971. Informal co-operation between other members of the team goes back to the late 1950s
Banco di Roma Commerzbank Crédit Lyonnais	33,156	1971	—	Representative offices in Johannesburg, Tokyo, Singapore, Mexico, Sydney	Described by the partner banks as a "quasi-merger"
Algemene Bank Nederland Banque de Bruxelles Bayerische Hypotheken-und-Wechselbank Dresdner Bank	29,006	1971	Associated Banks of Europe Corporation (ABECOR)	US investment bank/securities house; proposed representative offices in Johannesburg, Mexico, Sydney, and with other partners, Société Financiere Européenne (Paris)	Formed from the "inner ring" of partners in SFE plus Bayernhypo. Barclays, Banca Nazionale del Lavoro and Groupe BNP, the "outer ring", participate in group committees in specific fields. The other SFE partner, Bank of America, opted out altogether
Banco Ambrosiano (Milan) Berliner Handelsgesellshaft Frankfurter Bank Crédit Commercial de France Kredietbank (Antwerp) Nederlandsche Middenstandsbank Williams and Glyn's	9,985	1972	—	—	Association agreement to be known as the Inter-Alpha group

*$millions. 1971 balance sheet figures, almost all for end-year. EBIC assets exclude Banca Commerciale Italiana.

Table 6. "Other Banks" – Main Balance Sheet Items

	1965	1966	1967	1968	1969	1970	(£ millions) Mar. 1972
LIABILITIES							
Current and deposit accounts							
From UK banks:							
in sterling	41	54	133	302	456	570	1,145
in other currencies	39	39	145	215	528	669	858
From other UK residents:							
in sterling	143	152	352	565	613	754	1,514
in other currencies	1	4	20	14	29	27	45
From overseas residents:							
in sterling	35	48	57	60	73	81	245
in other currencies	59	61	173	290	582	835	1,175
Total deposits	**318**	**358**	**879**	**1,544**	**2,220**	**2,936**	**4,982**
ASSETS							
Balances with other UK banks	56	59	256	480	860	946	1,420
Money at call and short notice	11	15	12	15	25	96	363
Loans to UK local authorities	97	80	187	408	521	680	701
Sterling bills discounted	15	17	28	21	19	34	39
British Government Stocks	7	11	28	17	18	12	57
Advances to UK residents:							
in sterling	101	134	188	247	216	275	1,604
in other currencies	2	3	15	42	75	164	212
Advances to overseas residents:							
in sterling	6	7	14	13	18	13	48
in other currencies	36	44	139	283	687	1,041	1,484
Total advances	**144**	**188**	**355**	**586**	**996**	**1,493**	**3,348**
Other assets	11	14	48	64	84	167	370
Acceptances	16	16	18	21	16	16	23

*The banks whose business is reflected in this table are listed on pages 152–162. The figures are intended only as a guide to the main trends.

Table 7. Analysis of Advances by Banks in Great Britain (as at 17th May 1972)

(£ millions)

Category	London clearing banks	Scottish clearing banks	Accepting houses, overseas banks and other domestic banks	Total	% of total advances to UK residents
To UK residents					
Food, drink and tobacco	196	40	194	430	*3.5*
Chemicals and allied industries	137	8	194	338	*2.7*
Metal manufacture	105	9	58	172	*1.4*
Electrical engineering	227	10	113	350	*2.8*
Other engineering and metal goods	628	64	231	923	*7.4*
Shipbuilding	318	26	38	383	*3.1*
Vehicles	251	4	207	463	*3.7*
Textiles, leather and clothing	215	20	80	314	*2.5*
Other manufacturing	318	31	159	508	*4.1*
Total manufacturing	**2,395**	**212**	**1,274**	**3,881**	***31.2***
Other production:					
Agriculture, forestry and fishing	499	95	14	608	*4.9*
Mining and quarrying	36	2	163	201	*1.6*
Construction	559	33	80	672	*5.4*
Total other production	**1,093**	**130**	**257**	**1,481**	***11.9***
Financial:					
Hire purchase finance companies†	72	29	127	228	*1.8*
Property companies	444	37	296	776	*6.2*
United Kingdom banks†	88	16	116	220	*1.8*
Other financial	290	46	867	1,203	*9.7*
Total financial	**894**	**127**	**1,406**	**2,427**	***19.5***

(cont.)

Table 7. Analysis of Advances by Banks in Great Britain (as at May 1972)—cont.

(£ millions)

Category	London clearing banks	Scottish clearing banks	Accepting houses, overseas banks and other domestic banks	Total	% of total advances to UK residents
Services:					
Transport and communication	156	25	157	338	2.7
Public utilities (gas, electricity and water) and national government	140	21	79	241	1.9
Local government services†	26	10	26	62	0.4
Retail distribution	384	32	60	477	3.8
Other distribution	332	36	296	653	5.2
Professional, scientific and miscellaneous services	646	66	197	909	7.3
Total services	**1,675**	**190**	**815**	**2,679**	**21.5**
Personal:					
House purchase	478	23	101	602	4.8
Other personal	1,126	82	169	1,378	11.1
Total personal	**1,604**	**105**	**270**	**1,979**	**15.9**
Total to UK residents	**7,661**	**764**	**4,022**	**12,447**	
To Overseas residents† (including banks overseas)	**175**	**11**	**6,600**	**6,786**	
Total advances	**7,836**	**776**	**10,621**	**19,233***	
*Of which advances in foreign currencies to: UK residents				1,568	
overseas residents				6,347	
Total				**7,914**	

†Excluding funds placed through the specialised financial markets.

Table 8. Britain's Big Four Banking Groups – Main Subsidiary and Associated Banks

(Most of the banks have other interests, notably at home in such fields as unit trusts, insurance, trust services etc., in addition to those mentioned.)

1. Barclays Bank Group

	Per cent of equity held	Other participating banks and notes
International links		
Barclays Bank International	100	See Note 1
Barclays Bank (London & International)	100	Active in money markets and merchant banking
Barclays Bank SA, Paris	100	Operates branches in France
Barclays Bank of New York	—	Owned by Barclays Bank International
Barclays Bank of California	—	Barclays Bank International – 100 per cent: See Note 2
Société Financière Européenne (Luxembourg and Paris) (See Note 3)	14.3	Bank of America Algemene Bank Nederland Banca Nazionale del Lavoro Banque de Bruxelles Banque Nationale de Paris Dresdner Bank (all with 14.3 per cent)
Société Bancaire Barclays (Suisse)	—	51 per cent held by BBI
Domestic banking links		
Bank of Scotland	35	
Barclays Bank Trust Co.	100	
Yorkshire Bank	32	A bank operating in the north of England

Notes: 1. Barclays Bank International (formerly DCO) is an overseas bank with branches in the United States, Europe, and over 1,500 other branches in Africa, the Caribbean, the Mediterranean and Near East (often through subsidiaries).

2. Barclays Bank of California operates branches in California.

3. Société Financière Européenne provides services to European companies, partly through the provision of medium-term credit in Euro-currencies.

2. National Westminster Group

International links		
Orion Group (see Note 1)	21.5	Chase Manhattan Royal Bank of Canada – Westdeutsche Landesbank Girozentrale Credito Italiano Mitsubishi Bank

	Per cent of equity held	Other participating banks and notes
International Westminster Bank	100	See Note 2
Standard and Chartered Banking	9.2	Chase Manhattan National Bank of Abu Dhabi Midland Bank
Diners Club	49.7	Credit card organisation
RoyWest Banking Corporation	25	Royal Bank of Canada Hongkong & Shanghai Morgan Grenfell
Domestic links		
Ulster Bank	100	Bank operating mainly in Northern Ireland
County Bank	100	Merchant bank
Coutts and Co.	100	A clearing bank
Lombard North Central	100	Finance company
Credit Factoring	100	Factoring company
Yorkshire Bank	40	Bank operating in north of England

Notes: 1. Orion Bank and Orion Termbank were set up in 1971 as co-operative ventures by this group of large banks to help service international companies.

2. International Westminster Bank operates in sterling and Euro-currency money markets and has branches in France, Belgium and the Channel Islands.

3. Midland Bank Group

International links		
EBIC (European Banks International Company) (See Note 1)	16.7	Creditanstalt-Bankverein Deutsche Bank Société Generale de Banque Société Generale (France) Amsterdam-Rotterdam Bank Banca Commerciale Italiana
European-American Banks (New York)	20	See Note 2
Banque Européenne de Crédit à Moyen Terme, Brussels	14	See Note 4
Midland and International Banks (See Note 3)	45	Standard Bank – 19 per cent Commercial Bank of Australia – 10 per cent Toronto-Dominion Bank – 26 per cent
Euro-Pacific Finance Corp.,	17	Australia
UBAF Ltd. (Eurocurrency bank)	25	Union de Banques Arabes et Francaise Libyan Arab Foreign Bank
European-Asian Bank	17	EBIC group and others

	Per cent of equity held	Other participating banks and notes
Domestic links		
Montagu Trust	33⅓	Company which owns Samuel Montagu, the merchant bank
Clydesdale Bank	100	Scottish bank
Northern Bank	100	Bank operating mainly in Northern Ireland
Midland Bank Finance Corp.	100	
Forward Trust	100	Hire purchase finance company
Shield Factors	50	Factoring company
Midland Montagu Industrial Finance	50	Company development

Notes: 1. EBIC is a major co-operative grouping of European banks which are co-ordinating some of their international activities and conducting joint ventures (such as the bank in New York listed).

2. This is a joint venture in New York by the group of European banks brought together in EBIC.

3. Midland and International Banks is a London-based bank providing medium and long-term credit facilities. It is active in the London money markets.

4. A medium-term Eurocurrency lending bank owned jointly by the EBIC group, plus Samuel Montagu.

4. Lloyds Bank Group

International links		
Lloyds & Bolsa International	100	(See Note 1)
National Bank of New Zealand	100	Has 218 offices in New Zealand
National and Grindlays		(See Note 2)
Domestic links		
National and Commercial Banking Group	16.4	Scottish bank
Lloyds and Scottish	43.2	Finance house
Lloyds Associated Banking Co.	100	Active in sterling money markets and medium-term finance
Exporters Refinance Corporation	75.6	Hongkong & Shanghai Banking Corporation – 8.1 per cent National and Grindlays Bank – 16¼ per cent
Yorkshire Bank	20	Bank operating in north of England

Notes: 1. Lloyds and Bolsa International is an international bank with 36 banking offices in Europe, 124 in Latin America and 1 in USA.

2. Lloyds Bank holds 41 per cent of the equity of a holding company which, in its turn, owns 60 per cent of the equity of National and Grindlays Bank – a British Overseas Bank. First National City Bank of New York has a 40 per cent interest in National and Grindlays itself.

Table 9. The Big Four Deposit Banks in 1971

Main liabilities and balance sheet total of parent bank and group (consolidated accounts) December 1971

(£ millions)

	Deposits	Issued share capital	Reserves	Total assets	Profit (before tax)
Barclays Bank Limited	3,359	—	—	4,045	—
Barclays Group	6,384	97	398	7,316	91.1
National Westminster Bank Limited	3,727	—	—	4,200	—
National Westminster Group	6,068	105	279	6,648	83.8
Midland Bank Limited	3,127	—	—	3,449	—
Midland Group	4,067	65	212	4,468	52.0
Lloyds Bank Limited	2,317	—	—	2,622	—
Lloyds Group	4,105	65	246	4,490	58.4

Table 10. Accepting Houses Committee

Committee of representatives from seventeen leading merchant banks – the following banks provide members (most usually their chairmen):

Arbuthnot Latham & Company Limited	37 Queen Street, London, E.C.4
Baring Brothers & Company Limited	8 Bishopsgate, London, E.C.2
Wm. Brandt's Sons & Company Limited	36 Fenchurch Street, London, E.C.3
Brown, Shipley & Company Limited	Founders Court, Lothbury, London, E.C.2
Charterhouse Japhet & Thomasson Ltd.	1 Paternoster Row, St. Paul's, London, E.C.4
Antony Gibbs & Sons Limited	22 Bishopsgate, London, E.C.2
Guiness Mahon & Company Limited	3 Gracechurch Street, London, E.C.3
Hambros Bank Limited	41 Bishopsgate, London, E.C.2
Hill Samuel & Company Limited	100 Wood Street, London, E.C.2
Kleinwort, Benson Limited	20 Fenchurch Street, London, E.C.3
Lazard Brothers & Company Limited	11 Old Broad Street, London, E.C.2
Samuel Montagu & Company Limited	114 Old Broad Street, London, E.C.2
Morgan Grenfell & Company Limited	23 Great Winchester Street, London, E.C.2
Rea Brothers Limited	36–37 King Street, London, E.C.2
N. M. Rothschild & Sons	New Court, St. Swithin's Lane, London, E.C.4
J. Henry Schroder Wagg & Company Limited	120 Cheapside, London, E.C.2
S. G. Warburg & Company Limited (incorporating Seligman Brothers)	30 Gresham Street, London, E.C.2

Table 11. Accepting Houses – Main Balance Sheet Items

(£ millions)

	Dec. 1951	Dec. 1955	Dec. 1962	Dec. 1965	Dec. 1969	Dec. 1970	Mar. 1972
LIABILITIES							
Current and deposit accounts							
From UK banks:	55	71	102				
in sterling				87	222	209	319
in other currencies				103	319	461	578
From other UK residents:			215				
in sterling				423	739	845	1,032
in other currencies				19	75	82	88
From overseas residents:	81	82	346				
in sterling				141	117	162	189
in other currencies				257	871	1,013	1,025
Total deposits	**136**	**152**	**663**	**1,031**	**2,446**	**3,005**	**3,609***
ASSETS							
Balances with other UK banks (all currencies)	5	5	86	178	718	603	684
Money at call and short notice	57	60	76	74	96	245	253
Loans to UK local authorities	1	2	122	242	337	393	436
Sterling bills discounted	14	23	34	38	19	24	22
British Government Stocks	40	48	59	57	56	25	63
Advances to UK residents:	25	30	124				
in sterling				211	261	293	427
in other currencies				19	115	187	208
Advances to overseas residents:	14	17	217				
in sterling				18	25	24	33
in other currencies				222	696	1,017	1,024
Total advances	**39**	**46**	**341**	**470**	**1,097**	**1,521**	**1,692**
Other assets (all currencies)	15	12	48	101	241	275	393
Acceptances	93	97	186	279	340	375	352

*Including certificate of deposit of £293 millions in sterling and £86 millions in dollars.

Table 12. *British Overseas and Commonwealth Banks – Main Balance Sheet Items*

(£ millions)

	Dec. 1951	Dec. 1955	Dec. 1962	Dec. 1965	Dec. 1969	Dec. 1970	Mar. 1972
LIABILITIES							
Current and deposit accounts							
From UK banks:							
in sterling	112	99	172	135	309	376	480
in other currencies				191	664	999	1,138
From other UK residents:							
in sterling			156	237	379	366	494
in other currencies				26	65	86	80
From overseas residents:							
in sterling	346	387	806	672	594	651	929
in other currencies				417	1,774	2,761	3,067
Total deposits	**542**	**545**	**1,134**	**1,676**	**4,184**	**5,797**	**7,133***
ASSETS							
Balances with other UK banks	31	43	181	349	1,553	1,864	2,055
Money at call and short notice	134	112	115	99	60	109	244
Loans to UK local authorities	2	1	78	123	314	407	481
Sterling bills discounted	79	123	126	129	85	72	97
British Government Stocks	238	285	385	416	308	399	334
Advances to UK residents:							
in sterling	38	47	125	233	263	298	458
in other currencies				31	197	407	469
Advances to overseas residents:							
in sterling	97	70	322	226	130	150	204
in other currencies				292	1,422	2,098	2,709
Total advances	**174**	**120**	**457**	**782**	**2,012**	**2,953**	**3,840**
Other assets (all currencies)	9	12	23	70	195	486	453
Acceptances	79	26	51	99	100	134	134

*Including certificates of deposit of £501 millions in sterling and £443 millions in US dollars.

*Table 13. Foreign Banks in London – Growth of their Business**

(£ millions)

	American banks	"Foreign banks and affiliates"	Other foreign banks	**Total foreign**	British overseas, merchant banks and other banks	Deposit banks
Total Deposits						
1955	123	140	n.a.	**263**	697	(6,685)
1960	389	311	n.a.	**700**	1,191	(7,407)
1965	1,432	523	604	**2,599**	2,706	10,080
1967	5,301	649	1,023	**6,973**	4,642	11,082
1969	9,755	1,553	1,200	**12,508**	8,615	11,136
1972 (Mar.)	13,870	3,213	2,445	**19,528**	15,724	14,588
Deposits of Overseas Residents						
1955	36	120	n.a.	**156**	467	n.a.
1960	290	251	n.a.	**541**	805	n.a.
1965	1,010	357	449	**1,815**	1,581	429
1967	2,300	362	653	**3,315**	2,180	426
1969	5,909	864	781	**7,555**	4,078	418
1972 (Mar.)	8,278	2,032	1,446	**11,756**	6,610	927
Deposits of UK Residents†						
1955	27	12	n.a.	**39**	170	(6,685)
1960	100	60	n.a.	**160**	386	(7,407)
1965	197	41	50	**288**	849	9,651
1967	327	93	90	**510**	1,279	9,656
1969	458	99	45	**602**	2,236	10,718
1972 (Mar.)	580	162	46	**688**	3,253	12,569
Advances to UK Residents†						
1955	30	15	n.a.	**45**	77	(2,005)
1960	78	43	n.a.	**121**	118	(3,746)
1965	314	81	55	**449**	596	5,269
1967	374	123	47	**544**	774	5,710
1969	506	165	64	**735**	1,085	6,114
1972 (Mar.)	1,066	298	134	**1,498**	3,378	7,386

*During the past decade there have been several changes in definition and scope of the official figures on which the above table is based; the figures are intended to give a broad picture of the main trends. Figures include sums in sterling and foreign currencies.

†Figures for deposits *exclude* balances from other UK banks; and figures for advances *exclude* short-term loans to local authorities and the money market and balances with other banks.

Table 14. American Banks in UK – Main Balance Sheet Items

(£ millions)

	Dec. 1951	Dec. 1955	Dec. 1962	Dec. 1965	Dec. 1969	Dec. 1970	Mar. 1972
LIABILITIES							
Current and deposit accounts							
From UK banks:							
in sterling			12	35	263	281	362
in other currencies				190	2,204	2,474	3,144
From other UK residents:	21	27					
in sterling			79	155	249	295	375
in other currencies				42	209	226	205
From overseas residents:							
in sterling	35	38	363	160	124	214	360
in other currencies				849	5,785	7,115	7,918
Total deposits	**96**	**123**	**454**	**1,432**	**9,755**	**11,568**	**13,870***
ASSETS							
Balances with other UK banks	16	13	64	199	1,703	2,655	3,970
Money at call and short notice	2	28	23	39	30	61	173
Loans to UK local authorities	—	—	—	28	91	169	277
Sterling bills discounted	16	19	13	12	10	20	32
British Government Stocks	11	8	2	6	3	3	14
Advances to UK residents:							
in sterling	16	30	101	240	331	369	609
in other currencies				74	175	285	457
Advances to overseas residents:							
in sterling	10	18	248	20	15	11	43
in other currencies				805	7,358	7,888	8,021
Total advances	**34**	**67**	**349**	**1,139**	**7,879**	**8,553**	**9,130**
Other assets (all currencies)	—	—	2	14	43	41	101
Acceptances	17	13	31	68	135	125	114

*Including certificates of deposit of £467 millions in sterling and £1,038 millions in US dollars.

Table 15. *"Foreign Banks and Affiliates" – Main Balance Sheet Items*

(£ millions)

	Dec. 1951	Dec. 1955	Dec. 1962	Dec. 1965	Dec. 1969	Dec. 1970	Mar. 1972
LIABILITIES							
Current and deposit accounts							
From UK banks:	10	12	77				
in sterling				46	153	189	188
in other currencies				79	138	268	448
From other UK residents:			23				
in sterling				40	90	85	146
in other currencies				1	9	10	16
From overseas residents:	53	120	263				
in sterling				171	84	105	190
in other currencies				189	778	1,141	1,842
Total deposits	**75**	**140**	**362**	**523**	**1,553**	**2,132**	**3,213***
ASSETS							
Balances with other UK banks	12	12	191	79	674	853	1,086
Money at call and short notice	25	66	32	29	22	36	78
Loans to UK local authorities	1	3	71	62	67	69	58
Sterling bills discounted	14	20	14	11	14	14	21
British Government Stocks	11	11	9	8	9	9	25
Advances to UK residents:	9	15	51				
in sterling				76	122	137	218
in other currencies				6	43	70	80
Advances to overseas residents:	10	17	119				
in sterling				23	14	14	21
in other currencies				123	555	880	1,530
Total advances	**21**	**33**	**170**	**228**	**734**	**1,101**	**1,849**
Other assets (all currencies)	1	2	3	19	47	73	83
Acceptances	21	22	27	47	52	41	92

Source – Bank of England *Quarterly Bulletin.*
*Including certificates of deposit of £85 millions in sterling and £298 millions in US dollars.

Table 16. "Other Overseas Banks" – Main Balance Sheet Items

(£ millions)

	1965	1966	1967	1968	Dec. 1969	Dec. 1970	Mar. 1972
LIABILITIES							
Current and deposit accounts							
From UK banks:							
in sterling	22	46	58	75	81	70	90
in other currencies	83	133	221	224	263	485	850
From other UK residents:							
in sterling	49	52	87	47	34	30	43
in other currencies	2	2	3	3	11	15	3
From overseas residents:							
in sterling	176	142	133	105	87	84	97
in other currencies	273	344	520	711	695	755	1,349
Total deposits	**604**	**720**	**1,023**	**1,166**	**1,200**	**1,447**	**2,445***
ASSETS							
Balances with other UK banks	77	91	232	188	196	259	374
Money at call and short notice	31	26	29	23	17	16	51
Loans to UK local authorities	13	10	33	14	8	10	10
Sterling bills discounted	10	12	12	6	8	5	12
British Government Stocks	22	36	32	29	37	6	13
Advances to UK residents:							
in sterling	51	53	41	43	37	36	70
in other currencies	4	6	6	15	27	29	64
Advances to overseas residents:							
in sterling	85	66	37	47	35	19	19
in other currencies	308	397	563	683	655	948	1,700
Total advances	**448**	**521**	**648**	**788**	**754**	**1,032**	**1,853**
Other assets	21	38	72	152	202	111	177
Acceptances	149	132	176	204	212	199	195

Source – Bank of England *Quarterly Bulletin*.
*Including certificates of deposit of £6 million in sterling and £7 million in US dollars.

*Table 17. Foreign Banks in London**

(See also Table 23, p. 168, for a list of new Foreign Banks.)

Bank	Estd. in	Date of entry into London†	Status of representation	Approx. staff in London	Other foreign offices§§	Offices of overseas affiliated banks‡‡
EUROPE						
Belgium						
‡Banque Belge (*Société Générale de Banque*)	1934	1909	Subsidiary	202	—	—
Banque Belgo-Congolaise	1960	1914	Branch	20	—	4
Bulgaria						
Bulgarian Foreign Trade Bank	1964	1970	Rep. office	2	1	—
Cyprus						
‡Bank of Cyprus (London) (*Bank of Cyprus*)	1960	1955	Subsidiary (3 branches)	65	—	—
Czechoslovakia						
Zivnostenska Banka	1868	1922	Branch	42	—	—
France						
Banque de l'Indochine	1875	1920	Branch	100	68	80
Banque de Paris et des Pays Bas	1964	1964	Branch	35	n.a.	n.a.
‡British and Continental Banking Co. (*Union Financière et Minière*)	1926	1926	Subsidiary	40	—	n.a.
‡British and French Bank (*Banque Nationale de Paris*)	1966	1967	Subsidiary (2 branches)	275	73	127
Crédit Commercial de France	1894	1924	Rep. office	2	4	1
Crédit Industriel et Commercial	1859	1895	Branch	37	1	54
Crédit Lyonnais	1863	1870	3 branches, rep. office	184	180	100
Société Générale	1864	1871	Branch	199	14	69
Germany						
Bank für Gemeinwirtschaft	1958	1969	Rep. office	3	2	3
‖Dresdner Bank	1872	1967	Rep. office	6	20	9
Investitions- und Handels-Bank	1948	1959	Rep. office	2	—	—

For the explanation of symbols see the notes on page 161.
Banks that arrived in London in the course of 1972 are shown separately at the end of this table.

Table 17. Foreign Banks in London—(cont.)*

Bank	Estd. in	Date of entry into London†	Status of representation	Approx. staff in London	Other foreign offices§§	Offices of overseas affiliated banks‡‡
Greece						
‡Commercial Bank of the Near East (*Commercial Bank of Greece*)	1922	1922	Affiliate	34	—	—
National Bank of Greece	1841	1896	2 branches	87	11	7
Hungary						
National Bank of Hungary	n.a.	1969	Rep. office	n.a.	n.a.	n.a.
Irish Republic						
Allied Irish Banks	1825	1825	3 branches	28	5	—
Bank of Ireland	1783	1970	Rep. office††	7	1	—
§Italy						
Banca Commerciale Italiana	1894	1947	Branch	38	14	100
Banca Nazionale dell' Agricoltura	1921	1970	Rep. office	4	3	—
Banca Popolare di Novara	1871	1962	Rep. office	5	1	—
Banco di Napoli	1539	1946	Rep. office	5	8	4
Banco di Roma	1880	1946	Rep. office	6	11	5
Banco di Sicilia	1860	1955	Rep. office	6	7	2
Credito Italiano	1870	1947	Rep. office	6	7	2
Istituto Bancario San Paolo di Torino	1563	1960	Rep. office	4	3	—
‡Italian Economic Corp. (*Banca Nazionale del Lavoro*)	1913	1951	Subsidiary (Rep. office)	12	14	110
Monte dei Paschi di Siena	1472	1970	Rep. office	4	1	—
Netherlands						
Algemene Bank Nederland NV	1829	1858	2 branches	155	100	—
Portugal						
Banco Nacional Ultramarino	1864	1970	Rep. office	5	4	—
Banco Totta & Acores	1843	1969	Rep. office	5	2	—

For the explanation of symbols see the notes on page 161.

Table 17. Foreign Banks in London—(cont.)*

Bank	Estd. in	Date of entry into London†	Status of representation	Approx. staff in London	Other foreign offices§§	Offices of overseas affiliated banks‡‡
Spain						
Banco de Bilbao	1857	1918	4 branches	120	12	1
Banco de Santander	1857	1955	Rep. office	4	14	2
Banco Español de Credito	1902	1969	Rep. office	3	19	—
Banco Español en Londres	1951	1951	Affiliate (4 branches)	100	1	—
Banco Popular Español	1926	1968	Rep. office	2	21	50
Switzerland						
‡Julius Baer International (*Julius Baer & Co.*)	1890	1968	Affiliate	35	—	—
Crédit Suisse	1856	1954	Rep. office	5	14	1
Discount Bank (Overseas)	1952	1961	2 branches	35	3	—
Dow Banking Corporation	1965	1970	Branch	18	4	3
International Credit Bank, Geneva	1959	1963	Branch	40	10	1
Overseas Development Bank	1960	1967	Branch	23	2	—
Ralli Brothers (Bankers)***	1956	1971	Rep. office	n.a.	n.a.	n.a.
Swiss Bank Corporation	1872	1898	2 branches	n.a.	25	1
Swiss-Israel Trade Bank	1950	1956	Branch	81	3	8
Trade Development Bank	1960	1965	Branch	75	9	3
Union Bank of Switzerland	1862	1967	Branch	90	16	2
Yugoslavia						
Beogradska Banka	1971	1969	Rep. office	2	—	—
Yugoslav Bank for Foreign Trade	1955	1965	Rep. office	4	10	—
Yugoslav Investment Bank	1956	1969	Rep. office	2	7	—

For the explanation of symbols see the notes on page 161.

Table 17. Foreign Banks in London—(cont.)*

Bank	Estd. in	Date of entry into London†	Status of representation	Approx. staff in London	Other foreign offices§§	Offices of overseas affiliated banks‡‡
NORTH AMERICA						
Canada						
Bank of Montreal	1817	1870	2 branches	200	17	8
Bank of Nova Scotia	1832	1920	5 branches	182	113	45
Canadian Imperial Bank of Commerce	1867	1901	2 branches	106	58	18
Royal Bank of Canada	1869	1910	2 branches	315	125	32
Toronto-Dominion Bank	1856	1911	2 branches	65	9	5
United States						
Allied Bank International	1968	1969	Branch	17	3	—
American Express International Banking Corporation	1890	1920	Branch	130	48	—
American National Bank and Trust Company of Chicago	1928	1969	Branch	12	—	—
Bank of America	1904	1931	2 branches	430	200	60
Bank of California	1864	1971	Branch	15	3	—
Bank of New York	1784	1967	Branch	40	—	—
Bank of Tokyo Trust Co. (*Bank of Tokyo*)†††	1955	1971	Branch	12	—	—
Bankers Trust Company	1903	1922	2 branches	413	20	14
Chase Manhattan Bank	1799	1887	2 branches	575	90	2,042‖‖
Chemical Bank	1824	1960	2 branches	182	17	5
City National Bank of Detroit	1949	1968	Branch	19	—	—
Continental Illinois National Bank and Trust Company of Chicago	1857	1962	2 branches	129	25	13
Crocker National Bank	1870	1964	Branch	53	6	1
Detroit Bank & Trust Co.	1849	1969	Branch	17	1	—
Fidelity Bank	1866	1971	Rep. office	3	2	—

For the explanation of symbols see the notes on page 161.

Table 17. Foreign Banks in London—(cont.)*

Bank	Estd. in	Date of entry into London†	Status of representation	Approx. staff in London	Other foreign offices§§	Offices of overseas affiliated banks‡‡
Fiduciary Trust Co. of New York	1931	1965	Rep. office	5	1	—
First National Bank in Dallas	1875	1970	Branch	27	2	—
First National Bank of Boston	1784	1964	2 branches	135	23	—
First National Bank of Chicago	1863	1959	Branch	132	21	5
First National City Bank	1812	1902	2 branches	1,020	301	244
First Pennsylvania Banking and Trust Co.	1782	1968	Branch	30	2	1
First Wisconsin National Bank of Milwaukee	1853	1968	Branch	30	—	—
Franklin National Bank	1926	1969	Rep. office	4	1	10
Girard Trust Bank	1836	1968	Branch	32	1	—
Harris Trust and Savings Bank	1882	1970	Branch	27	—	—
International Bank of Washington	1920	1970	Rep. office	2	15	2
Irving Trust Company	1851	1965	Branch	90	10	2
La Salle National Bank	1927	1971	Rep. office	2	1	—
Manufacturers Hanover Trust Co.	1831	1925	2 branches	360	16	2
Marine Midland Bank-New York	1907	1964	Branch	85	12	7
Mellon National Bank and Trust Company	1869	1968	Branch	70	2	1
Morgan Guaranty Trust Company of New York	1828	1892	2 branches	455	18	23
National Bank of Detroit	1933	1968	Branch	32	1	2
National Bank of Commerce of Seattle	1889	1968	Branch	25	8	—
Northern Trust Company	1889	1969	Branch	38	—	—
Philadelphia National Bank	1803	1969	Rep. office	3	1	—
Republic National Bank of Dallas	1920	1970	Branch	25	3	—
Security Pacific National Bank	1871	1969	Branch	65	8	2
United California Bank	1868	1968	Branch	57	8	4
Wells Fargo Bank	1852	1969	Rep. office	8	9	5

For the explanation of symbols see the notes on page 161.

Table 17. Foreign Banks in London—(cont.)*

Bank	Estd. in	Date of entry into London†	Status of representation	Approx. staff in London	Other foreign offices§§	Offices of overseas affiliated banks‡‡
REST OF THE WORLD						
Afghanistan						
‡Afghan National Bank (*Banke Millie Afghan*)	1932	1935	Subsidiary	4	5	—
Argentina						
Banco de Galicia y Buenos Aires	1905	1969	Rep. office	3	—	—
Australia						
Bank of Adelaide	1865	1890	Branch	75	—**	—
Bank of New South Wales	1817	1853	3 branches	500	4**	1
Commercial Bank of Australia	1866	1882	2 branches	167	3**	—
Commercial Banking Co. of Sydney	1834	1859	2 branches	130	—**	1
Commonwealth Trading Bank of Australia	1911	1913	3 branches	217	1**	—
National Bank of Australasia	1858	1864	3 branches	235	2**	—
Bahamas						
Butlers Bank	1962	1968	Rep. office	2	5	—
Bank of New Providence	1965	1969	Branch	4	—	—
Deltec Banking Corp.	1961	1964	Rep. office	20	13	3
Barbados						
Caribbean National Bank	1967	1967	Branch	6	—	—
Bermuda						
‡B of B (Europe) (*Bank of Bermuda*)	1890	1968	Subsidiary (Rep. office)	3	—	—
N. T. Butterfield & Son (Bermuda) (*Bank of N. T. Butterfield & Son*)	1858	1964	Subsidiary (Rep. office)	6	—	—
Brazil						
Banco do Brasil	1808	1970	Branch	17	9	—

For the explanation of symbols see the notes on page 161.

Table 17. Foreign Banks in London—(cont.)*

Bank	Estd. in	Date of entry into London†	Status of representation	Approx. staff in London	Other foreign offices§§	Offices of overseas affiliated banks‡‡
Banco do Estado de Sao Paulo	1926	1970	Branch	14	2	—
Ceylon						
Bank of Ceylon	1939	1949	Branch	22	—	—
China						
Bank of China	1912	1929	Branch	110	8	—
Cuba						
Banco Nacional de Cuba	1948	1968	Rep. office	10	1	—
Ghana						
Ghana Commercial Bank	1953	1959	Branch	70	2	—
Hong Kong						
‡British Bank of the Middle East (*Hongkong and Shanghai*)	Inc. in London 1889		Subsidiary	212	49	18
‡Hongkong and Shanghai Banking Corporation	1865	1865	2 branches	598	70	—
Mercantile Bank (*Hongkong and Shanghai*)	Inc. in London 1892		Subsidiary	90	52	—
India						
Bank of Baroda	1908	1957	2 branches	100	17	—
Bank of India	1906	1946	Branch	60	13	3
Central Bank of India	1911	1953	Branch	40	—	—
State Bank of India	1955	1921	Branch	96	4	—
United Commercial Bank	1943	1953	Branch	45	8	—
Indonesia						
Bank Indonesia	1953	1958	Rep. office	7	4	—
Bank Negara Indonesia	1946	1971	Rep. office	4	4	—
Iran						
Bank Bazargani Iran	1950	1956	Rep. office	4	1	—

For the explanation of symbols see the notes on page 161.

Table 17. Foreign Banks in London—(cont.)*

Bank	Estd. in	Date of entry into London†	Status of representation	Approx. staff in London	Other foreign offices§§	Offices of overseas affiliated banks‡‡
Bank Melli Iran	1928	1967	2 branches	51	7	1
Bank Saderat Iran	1952	1963	Branch	13	14	—
Bank Sepah-Iran	1925	1970	Rep. office	3	—	—
Iraq						
Rafidain Bank	1941	1954	Branch	49	3	1
Israel						
‡Anglo-Israel Bank (*Bank Leumi le-Israel*)	1959	1959	Subsidiary	95	—	—
Bank Hapoalim	1921	1969	Branch	15	4	2
Export Bank	1935	1961	Rep. office	2	2	—
‡Israel-British Bank (London) (*Israel-British Bank*)	1968	1945	Subsidiary	50	—	—
Japan§						
Bank of Kobe	1936	1956	Branch	15	3	—
Bank of Tokyo	1946	1952	Branch	200	77	27
Dai-Ichi Kangyo Bank	1971	1958	Branch	46	12	3
Daiwa Bank	1918	1958	Branch	22	3	1
Fuji Bank	1866	1952	Branch	47	7	—
Hokkaido Takushoku Bank	1900	1971	Rep. office	3	1	—
Industrial Bank of Japan	1902	1964	Branch	18	3	7
Kyowa Bank	1945	1970	Rep. office	3	1	—
Long-Term Credit Bank of Japan	1952	1971	Rep. office	3	1	1
Mitsubishi Bank	1919	1956	Branch	40	8	2
Mitsui Bank	1876	1952	Branch	42	8	3
Saitama Bank	1943	1971	Rep. office	3	1	1
Sanwa Bank	1933	1957	Branch	35	6	—
Sumitomo Bank	1895	1956	Branch	35	21	1

For the explanation of symbols see the notes on page 161.

Table 17. Foreign Banks in London—(cont.)*

Bank	Estd. in	Date of entry into London†	Status of representation	Approx. staff in London	Other foreign offices§§	Offices of overseas affiliated banks‡‡
Tokai Bank	1941	1963	Branch	28	4	2
Korea						
Korea Exchange Bank	1967	1967	Branch	21	17	—
Kuwait						
‡United Bank of Kuwait	1966	1966	Priv co	85	—	—
Malaysia						
Malayan Banking Berhad	1960	1962	Branch	13	113	—
Mexico						
Banco de Comercio	1932	1970	Rep. office	5	2	—
New Zealand						
Bank of New Zealand	1861	1862	3 branches	185	13	1
Nigeria						
African Continental Bank	1946	1961	Branch	15	—	—
National Bank of Nigeria	1933	1956	Branch	37	—	—
Pakistan						
Habib Bank (Overseas)	1952	1961	2 branches	76	16	1
Muslim Commercial Bank	1948	1965	Branch	32	3	—
National Bank of Pakistan	1949	1954	Branch	65	6	—
Pakistan Overseas Standard Bank	1963	1968	Branch	11	1	—
United Bank	1959	1963	2 branches	63	24	—
Philippines						
Philippine National Bank	1916	1968	Rep. office	5	9	—
Singapore						
Oversea-Chinese Banking Corporation	1932	1969	Branch	9	30	—
Overseas Union Bank	1949	1963	Branch	21	16	—

For the explanation of symbols see the notes on page 161.

Table 17. Foreign Banks in London—(cont.)*

Bank	Estd. in	Date of entry into London†	Status of representation	Approx. staff in London	Other foreign offices§§	Offices of overseas affiliated banks‡‡
South Africa						
‡French Bank of Southern Africa (*Banque de l'Indochine*)	1949	1963	Branch	12	1	—
Nedbank	1888	1906	2 branches	119	11	6
Trust Bank of Africa	1954	1971	Rep. office	2	—	—
Western Acceptances (*Western Bank*)	n.a.	1971	Subsidiary	n.a.	n.a.	n.a.
Thailand						
Bangkok Bank	1944	1957	Branch	42	15	—
Turkey						
Ottoman Bank	1863	1863	Branch	5	20	—
U.S.S.R.						
Moscow Narodny Bank	1919	1916	Priv co	260	2	—

Source: *The Banker*, London, November 1971.

*Including Commonwealth banks but excluding central banks and British-owned members of the British and Commonwealth Banks Association with head offices in London.

†Date given for entry into London may in some cases refer to the year in which the bank's forerunner opened a branch or representative office.

‡Denotes banks that are registered in the UK, but in which non-UK residents hold a controlling interest. The parent bank is shown in italics.

||The forerunner of the present Dresdner Bank maintained a full branch in the City before World War 1 – as did its two other main competitors at that time, Deutsche Bank and Disconto Gesellschaft.

§Dates given under the column "Date of entry into London" are those for the opening of offices after World War 2; three Italian banks were represented in London before the war – Credito Italiano, Banco di Roma and Banca Commerciale Italiana – when they maintained full branches, as did also a number of Japanese banks.

**Excluding offices in Australasia.

††This bank which, like the Allied Irish Group, also operates in Northern Ireland, has opened two full branches in London City and Shepherds Bush.

‡‡Approximate figure for offices of overseas banking institutions, excluding London, in which 10 to 50 per cent is held.

§§Including approximate figures for offices of banking subsidiaries overseas.

|| ||Including offices of Standard and Chartered Group (over 900 in South Africa alone).

***Formerly associated with the UK Ralli Brothers, but there is now no shareholding link.

†††US-incorporated subsidiary of the Japanese bank.

*Table 18. Foreign Banks with Minority Interests in British Banks**

Foreign bank	Country	% of capital	Year share-holding taken	British bank and address	Other main partners and % shareholdings	
Chase Manhattan	USA	13.77	1965	Standard and Chartered Banking Group	National Westminster Midland Bank	(9.18) (4.59)
First National City Bank	USA	40.0	1969	National & Grindlays Bank	Lloyds Bank Ltd.	(24.72)
First National Bank of Chicago	USA	20.0	1972	Commercial Bank of Wales	The Hodge Group Sun Alliance Hambros	(16.0) (4.0) (2.0)
First National Bank of Maryland	USA	25.0	1970	First Maryland Ltd.	Stern Holdings Ltd.	(75.0)
Franklin National Bank	USA	10.0	1970	Sterling Industrial Securities Ltd.	Crown Agents N. M. Rothschild and Sons Ltd. Eagle Star Insurance Co. Ltd.	(26.6) (10.0) (8.3)
International Bank of Washington	USA	50.0	1965	Security Trust Co. of Birmingham	Interests of Sir Isaac Wolfson Bt.	(50.0)
Mellon Bank International	USA	12.63	1971	Lloyds and Bolsa International Bank	Lloyds Bank Ltd.	(55.44)
Morgan Guaranty	USA	32.0	1936	Morgan Grenfell & Co.	None	
Philadelphia National Bank	USA	9.9	1965	Arbuthnot Latham Holdings Ltd.	ICFC Chartered Bank Pearl Assurance	(24.4) (9.5) (9.2)
Texas Commerce Bank	USA	35.0	1968	Burston and Texas Commerce Bank	Burston Group Ltd.	(65.0)

*Banks with majority of capital British owned.

Table 19. Euro-currency Consortia Banks, June 1972

Bank	Year set up	Total assets (£'000s end 1971)	Loans (£'000) over 1 year	Partners and per cent shareholding
Midland and International Banks, London	1964	491,313*	139,698*	Midland Bank (45), Toronto Dominion (26), Standard Bank (19), Commercial Bank of Australia (10).
Western American Bank, London	1968	396,725†	192,542†	Hambros Bank (28), National Bank of Detroit (24), Security Pacific, (24), Wells Fargo (24).
International Commercial Bank, London	1967	316,121	112,662	Commerzbank (25), First National Bank of Chicago (25), Hongkong & Shanghai (25), Irving Trust (25).
Banque Européenne de Crédit à Moyen Terme, Brussels	1967	278,732	128,510	Amsterdam-Rotterdam Bank (14.05), Banca Commerciale Italiana (14.05), Deutsche Bank (14.05), Midland Bank (14.05), Société Générale (14.05), Société Générale de Banque (14.05), Samuel Montagu (3.6), Creditanstalt Bankverein (7.1).
Rothschild Intercontinental Bank, London	1969‡	185,776§	69,156§	N. M. Rothschild & Sons (28), First City National Bank of Houston (11.7), Industrial Bank of Japan (11.7), National City Bank of Cleveland (11.7), Seattle First National Bank (11.7), Banque Rothschild (6.5), Pierson Heldring & Pierson, Amsterdam (6.5), Banque Lambert Brussels (6.5), Sal Oppenheim, Jnr. (6.36), Banque Privée, Geneva (2.5).
Orion Termbank, London	1971	156,623	52,999	Chase Manhattan (21.5), National Westminster Bank (21.5), Royal Bank of Canada (21.5), Westdeutsche Landesbank Girozentrale (21.5), Credito Italiano (7), Mitsubishi Bank (7).
Scandinavian Bank, London	1969	149,432	48,723	Skandinaviska Enskilda Banken (34.8), Bergens Privatbank (19.4), Pohjoismaiden Yhdyspankki/Nordiska Föreningsbanken (19.4), Den Danske Landmandsbank (14.5), Den Danske Provinsbank (4.8), Skanska Banken (3.9), Landsbanki Islands (3.2).
Société Financière Européenne, Paris	1967	124,083‖	n.a.	Algemene Bank Nederland (14.3), Banca Nazionale del Lavoro (14.3), Bank of America (14.3), Banque de Bruxelles (14.3), Barclays Bank (14.3), Dresdner Bank (14.3), Groupe BNP (14.3).
London Multinational Bank, London	1970	121,113**	29,663**	Chemical International Banking Co. (30), Crédit Suisse (30), Baring Bros. (20), Northern Trust (20).

Table 19. Euro-currency Consortia Banks, June 1972

Bank	Year set up	Total assets (£'000s end 1971)	Loans (£'000) over 1 year	Partners and per cent shareholding
Banque Européenne de Tokyo, Paris	1968	91,585§	n.a.	Bank of Tokyo (29.6), Industrial Bank of Japan (29.6), Bank of Tokyo, Luxembourg (14.8), Long Term Credit Bank of Japan (11.08), Bank of Kobe (3.73), Kyowa Bank (3.73), Nippon Fudosan Bank (3.73), Saitama Bank (3.73).
Associated Japanese Bank (International), London	1970	77,621††	n.a.	Dai-Ichi Kangyo Bank (25), Mitsui Bank (25), Nomura Securities (25), Sanwa Bank (25).
Japan International Bank, London	1971	51,689	14,282	Fuji Bank (20), Mitsubishi Bank (20), Sumitomo Bank (20), Tokai Bank (20), Daiwa Securities (6.6), Nikko Securities (6.6), Yamaichi Securities (6.6).
Nordic Bank, London	1971	51,158	7,002	Den Norske Creditbank (33.33), Kansallis-Osake-Pankki (33.33), Svenska Handelsbanken (33.33).
United International Bank, London	1970	45,312	12,157	Banco di Roma (10), Bank Mees & Hope, Netherlands (10), Bank of Nova Scotia (10), Banque Française du Commerce Exterieur (10), Bayerische Hypotheken-und Wechselbank (10), Crédit du Nord (10), Crocker National Bank (10), Privatbanken i Kjobenhavn (10), Sveriges Kreditbank (10), Williams & Glyns (10).
Atlantic International Bank, London	1969	44,137‡‡	21,991‡‡	Banco di Napoli (12.5), Banque de Neuflize, Schlumberger, Mallet, Paris (12.5), Charterhouse Japhet (12.5), First Pennsylania Overseas Corp. (12.5), F. Van Lanschot (12.5), Manufacturers National Bank of Detroit (12.5), National Shawmut Bank of Boston (12.5), United California Bank (12.5).
London Interstate Bank, London	1971	40,900§§	n.a.	First National Bank, Atlanta (16.7), First Western Bank & Trust Co., Los Angeles (16.7), Indiana National Bank (16.7), Keyser Ullmann (16.7), Maryland National Bank (16.7), Mercantile Trust Co., St. Louis (16.7).
Interunion-Banque, Paris	1969	24,423	n.a.	Banque de l'Union Européenne et Compagne Financière de l'Union Européenne Paris (20), Marine Midland Banks (20), Banque de Bruxelles (10), Bayerische Vereinsbank (10), Royal Bank of Canada International, Nassau (10), Société Financiere Desmarais pour l'Industrie et le Commerce (FDIC), Paris (10), Banque Commerciale de Bâle (5), Banque Belge pour l'Industrie (5), Hambros Bank (5), La Centrale Finanziara Generale, Milan (5).

Source: *The Banker*, June 1972.
*End March 1971. †End January 1972, consolidated figures. ‡Formerly National Provincial and Rothschild. §End September 1971. ||End 1970.
**End October 1971. ††End February 1972. ‡‡End June 1971. §§End March 1972.

Table 20. Discount Market – Sources of Borrowed Funds

(£ millions)

End of	Bank of England	London clearing banks	Scottish banks and other deposit banks	"Wholesale" banks*	Other sources	Total
1958	8	519	169	263	47	**1,006**
1963	4	688	114	265	162	**1,232**
1965	34	849	145	242	111	**1,381**
1966	82	978	105	201	119	**1,484**
1967	116	1,076	123	218	136	**1,662**
1968	—	1,132	115	204	121	**1,573**
1969	—	1,304	110	202	109	**1,725**
1970	—	1,407	137	510	204	**2,259**
1971	76	1,241	131	1,116	398	**2,961**
1972 (June 21)	—	702	136	999	522	**2,361**

*Accepting houses, overseas and foreign banks and other banks.

Table 21. Discount Market Assets

End of	Government securities		Treasury bills		Commercial and other sterling bills		Local authority securities	Other assets	Total	Certificates of deposit Sterling	Certificates of deposit US dollars
	£m.	Per cent of total	£m.	Per cent of total	£m.	Per cent of total	£m.	£m.		£	£
1958	321	30	594	56	70	7	—	68	**1,053**	—	—
1963	442	34	529	41	249	19	—	84	**1,305**	—	—
1965	500	34	484	33	339	23	—	132	**1,455**	—	—
1966	542	35	424	27	404	26	—	195	**1,565**	—	—
1967	544	31	548	31	437	25	115	89	**1,747**	—	14
1968	306	18	471	28	560	34	148	83	**1,663**	56	39
1969	364	20	399	22	629	34	192	104	**1,817**	97	31
1970	160	7	876	37	697	30	224	88	**2,352**	268	39
1971	391	12	871	28	586	19	478	174	**3,066**	457	108
1972 (June 21)	307	12	357	15	374	15	511*	438*	**2,461**	469	111

*Local authority securities other than bonds included in "other assets".

Table 22. Interest Rates per cent per annum (end of period)

	1964	1965	1966	1967	1968	1969	1970	1971	(June) 1972
Bank Rate	7.00	6.00	7.00	8.00	7.00	8.00	7.00	5.00	6.00
Clearing banks:									
deposit rate	5.00	4.00	5.00	6.00	5.00	6.00	5.00	2.50	4.00
call money rate*	5.375	4.375	5.375	6.25	5.375	6.375	5.375	1.50	2.00
Treasury bills (yield)	6.74	5.60	6.64	7.62	6.90	7.80	6.93	4.46	5.27
Bank bills (3 months)	6.84	5.91	6.91	7.78	7.28	8.75	8.00	4.50	6.75
Deposits with local authorities:									
(7 days)	8.00	6.25	7.38	8.44	7.25	8.875	6.75	4.25	7.50
(3 months)	7.69	6.38	7.28	7.63	7.75	9.00	7.25	4.50	7.75
Deposits with finance houses:									
(3 months)	7.69	6.56	7.38	8.19	7.75	9.50	7.75	4.375	7.25
(6 months)	7.63	6.75	7.44	8.25	8.00	9.65	8.25	4.65	7.25
Euro-dollar deposits									
(3 months)	4.50	5.25	7.75	6.31	7.13	8.53	10.56	10.00	5.65
Inter-bank:									
(overnight lending)	n.a.	n.a.	6.50	8.25	6.75	2.75	6.00	1—5	5.00
(3 months)	n.a.	n.a.	7.25	8.25	8.00	9.50	7.25	4.50	7.65

*Minimum rates fixed until September 1971 at $1\frac{5}{8}$ below Bank Rate.

Table 23. *New Foreign Banks in London*

(The following list shows which foreign banks established themselves in London in the year to November 1972.)

Branches	*Country*
Pubali Bank	Bangladesh
Uttara Bank	Bangladesh
Janata Bank	Bangladesh
Commercial Bank of Malawi	Malawi
North Carolina National Bank	USA

Representative offices	
Banque Louis Dreyfus	France
Banca d'America et d'Italia	Italy
Istituto Mobiliare Italiano	Italy
Rumanian Bank for Foreign Trade	Rumania
Banco Urquijo	Spain
Investiciona Banka Titograd	Yugoslavia
Bishops Bank and Trust Co.	Nassau
First City National Bank of Houston	USA
First National Bank of Miami	USA
Houston Citizen Bank & Trust Co.	USA
Manufacturers National Bank of Detroit	USA
Northwestern National Bank of Minneapolis	USA
Republic National Bank of New York	USA
Texas Commerce Bank	USA
Union Commerce Bank	USA
Sterling Bank & Trust Co.	Cayman Islands
Israel Discount Bank	Israel
Sumitomo Trust and Banking	Japan
Mitsubishi Trust and Banking	Japan
Mitsui Trust and Banking	Japan
Nippon Fudosan Bank	Japan

Representative offices made into full Branches	*Staff* 1971	1972
Bank of Ireland	28	70
Credito Italiano	6	36
Crédit Suisse	5	25
Fidelity Bank	3	20
Franklin National Bank	4	30
Bank Sepah-Iran	3	15
Kyowa Bank	3	16

Index